sushi

sushi

MORE THAN 60 SIMPLE-TO-FOLLOW RECIPES

RYLAND PETERS & SMALL
LONDON • NEW YORK

Designer Paul Stradling
Editor Abi Waters
Production Manager Gordana Simakovic
Head of Production Patricia Harrington
Creative Director Leslie Harrington
Editorial Director Julia Charles

Indexer Cathy Heath

First published in 2024
by Ryland Peters & Small
20–21 Jockey's Fields
London WC1R 4BW
and
341 E 116th St
New York, NY 10029

www.rylandpeters.com

10 9 8 7 6 5 4 3 2 1

Text © Jordan Bourke, Maxine Clark, Amy
Ruth Finegold, Nicola Graimes, Dunja Gulin,
Tori Haschka, Emi Kazuko, Loretta Liu, Uyen Luu,
James Porter, Annie Rig, Fiona Smith, Milli Taylor,
Jenna Zoe and Ryland Peters & Small 2024
(Also see page 160 for full credits.)

Design and commissioned photographs
© Ryland Peters & Small 2024.
Cover illustration: Adobe Stock/Billy

ISBN 978-1-78879-582-1

A CIP record for this book is available from
the British Library.
US Library of Congress cataloging-in-publication
data has been applied for.

Printed in China

notes

- All spoon measurements are level unless otherwise specified.
- Eggs are medium unless otherwise specified. Uncooked or partly cooked eggs should not be served to the very young, the very old, those with compromised immune systems, or to pregnant women.
- Weights and measurements have been rounded up or down slightly to make measuring easier.
- When a recipe calls for the grated zest of a citrus fruit, buy unwaxed fruit and wash well before using. If you can only find treated fruit, scrub well in warm soapy water before using.
- Ovens should be preheated to the specified temperature. If using a fan-assisted oven, cooking times should be reduced according to the manufacturer's instructions.
- Japanese ingredients are now widely available in larger supermarkets, natural food stores and Asian markets.

contents

introduction

The food of the East has become so popular in recent years – and it's no surprise. From fresh fish and soft rice that melts in the mouth, to a warming, aromatic bowl of Vietnamese pho or a crisp salad, these are dishes packed full of bold flavours and ingredients that promote well-being. They have become the healthy, convenience food of our time, with more and more restaurants serving Asian-inspired dishes popping up.

But dishes such as sushi and noodle broths are also so simple to make at home and the ingredients are becoming more widely known and available. Even if you aren't lucky enough to have an Asian supermarket nearby, most of the ingredients are now universally available online.

While noodles are the fast food of Asia – quick, instantly satisfying and wholesome – it is sushi that has really come into it's own in recent years. For so long there was a mystique surrounding sushi that prevented it being a favourite with home cooks. But the complicated techniques used in making sushi can be simplified for the home and many people are now realizing how fun it can be to prepare – and how versatile too. Sushi is perfect for so many occasions, whether it's a healthy, convenient packed-lunch box or an elegant platter to serve to dinner guests. One of the most popular styles is rolled sushi (*maki-zushi*), which is the focus of the second chapter. As soon as the process of rolling the rice has been mastered, a world of filling options becomes available.

sushi-making utensils and ingredients

Special sushi-making utensils and authentic ingredients are beautiful and useful, and sold even in supermarkets. Many brands of nori are available pretoasted and in a variety of grades – use the best you can. Some of the recipes in this book call for only half a sheet. When this is so, cut the sheets in half from the shortest side, so you are left with the most width.

When making rolled sushi, remember that rice is easier to handle with wet hands and it is better to handle nori with dry. Keep a bowl of vinegared water (mix 60 ml/¼ cup rice vinegar into 250 ml/1 cup water) on hand to make the job easier. You can use a dish towel lined with a piece of clingfilm/plastic wrap to help roll sushi, but it is definitely worth investing in a rolling mat (*makisu*) – they are inexpensive and will make the process far easier.

serving sushi

Traditional accompaniments for sushi are soy sauce, wasabi paste and pickled ginger, and it is often served with miso soup. A smear of wasabi can elevate a piece of sushi from the ordinary to something truly extraordinary.

If you do not want to add wasabi in the sushi, serve a small mound on the side, or serve the sushi with a small dish of plain soy and one of wasabi and soy mixed together. Bought wasabi varies immensely; it is possible to find paste with a high percentage of real wasabi, but many are mostly horseradish – once again, buy the best you can or make your own for the best flavour (see page 18).

Sushi is traditionally served immediately, but if you have to keep it for a while, wrap uncut rolls in clingfilm/plastic wrap. Keep in a cool place, but NOT in the refrigerator, which will make the rice hard and unpleasant – the vinegar in the rice will help to preserve it for a short time.

With easy to follow recipes and step-by-step instructions, you can have so much fun experimenting with a whole range of exciting combinations. Just remember, when it comes to sushi, practice really does make perfect!

ingredients

mirin
Japanese sweet rice
wine, for cooking only

su
Japanese
rice vinegar

sake
Japanese
rice wine

shoyu
Japanese soy sauce

nori
sheets of dried
seaweed

kanpyo
dried gourd ribbons

kombu
dried kelp for
cooking rice

white sesame seeds

black sesame seeds

renkon, sliced
lotus root

shiso leaf
Japanese herb, also
known as perilla

Japanese ingredients are becoming more widely available in supermarkets
and specialist food stores, but can certainly be found in Asian markets.
This directory will help you identify them.

fresh ginger

abura-age
fried bean curd

takuan
pickled daikon radish

**Japanese
short-grained
sushi rice**

umeboshi
pickled red plums

**ready-made
pickled ginger**

wasabi paste
also available as
powder in tins

shiitake
dried mushrooms;
also available fresh

1 basics

vinegared rice

Sushi is a general term for all food with *sumeshi*, or vinegared rice. Remember – sushi should never be put in the fridge (it will go hard). The vinegar will help preserve it for a few days if kept, wrapped, in a cool place, such as a shady window sill. To make sushi rice, boil 15 per cent more water than rice. Don't take the lid off during cooking or you will spoil the rice.

400 ml/1¾ cups Japanese rice*

1 piece of dried kelp (*kombu*), 5 cm/2 inches square, for flavouring (optional)

3 tablespoons Japanese rice vinegar

2½ tablespoons sugar

2 teaspoons sea salt

makes 1 litre/4 cups

*Please note, the rice in this recipe is measured by volume, not weight.

Put the rice in a large bowl and wash it thoroughly, changing the water several times, until the water is clear. Drain and leave in the strainer for 1 hour. If short of time, soak the rice in clear cold water for 10–15 minutes, then drain.

Transfer to a deep, heavy-based saucepan, add 460 ml/2 cups water and a piece of dried kelp (*kombu*), if using. Cover and bring to the boil over a high heat for about 5 minutes. Discard the kelp.

Lower the heat and simmer, covered, for about 10 minutes, or until all the water has been absorbed. Do not lift the lid. Remove from the heat and leave, still covered, for about 10–15 minutes.

Mix the rice vinegar, sugar and salt in a small jug/pitcher and stir until dissolved.

Transfer the cooked rice to a large, shallow dish or *handai* (Japanese wooden sumeshi tub). Sprinkle generously with the vinegar dressing.

Using a wooden spatula, fold the vinegar dressing into the rice. Do not stir. While folding, cool the rice quickly using a fan. Let the rice cool to body temperature before using to make sushi.

japanese omelette

This is the basic method for cooking Japanese omelette (*tamago yaki*). In Japan it is a regular breakfast item as well as being used for sushi.

4 eggs

1 egg yolk

2½ tablespoons sugar

1 teaspoon Japanese soy sauce (shoyu)

sea salt

1–2 tablespoons sunflower oil

1 Japanese omelette pan or 20-cm/8-inch non-stick frying pan/skillet

chopsticks (hashi) or fork

makes 1 omelette

Using a fork, beat the eggs and egg yolk and strain through a sieve into a bowl. Add the sugar, soy sauce and a pinch of salt and stir well until the sugar has dissolved. Do not whisk or make bubbles.

Heat a Japanese omelette pan or frying pan/skillet over moderate heat and add a little oil. Spread evenly over the base by tilting the pan, then wipe off excess oil with kitchen paper, at the same time making sure the surface is absolutely smooth. Keep the oiled paper on a plate.

Lower the heat and pour one-third of the egg mixture evenly over the base by tilting the pan. If large air bubbles pop up immediately, the pan may be too hot – then remove the pan from the heat and put it back on when the egg starts to set.

Prick any air bubbles with a fork and when the egg is about to set, using chopsticks or a fork, roll the egg layer 2–3 times from one side to the other. Oil the empty base of the pan with the oiled paper and push the rolled egg back to the other side.

Again using the oiled paper, brush the base of the pan, then pour half the remaining egg mixture evenly over the base by tilting the pan and lifting the egg roll so the egg mixture flows underneath.

When the egg starts to set, roll again, using the first roll as the core. Repeat this oiling and rolling using up the remaining egg mixture. Remove from the pan and let cool before cutting.

mixed pickles

½ cucumber, about 10 cm/
4 inches long

1 carrot, about 100 g/4 oz.

100 g/4 oz. daikon radish,
peeled, or 6 red radishes

¼ small green cabbage, about
150 g/5 oz.

6 garlic cloves, finely sliced

1 tablespoon salt

½ lemon, sliced

250 ml/1 cup rice vinegar

175 g/1 cup sugar

makes about 500 ml/2 cups

Other vegetables can be pickled and served with sushi alongside ginger (see below). They look wonderfully colourful, adding a touch of drama to your sushi platter and making it appear very professional.

Cut the cucumber in half lengthways and scoop out the seeds. Slice the cucumber, carrot and radish into very thin strips.

Slice the cabbage into 1-cm/½-inch strips. Put all the vegetables and garlic in a colander, sprinkle with salt and toss well. Set aside for 30 minutes, then rinse thoroughly and top with the sliced lemon.

Put the rice vinegar and sugar in a saucepan with 60 ml/¼ cup water. Bring to the boil, stirring until the sugar has dissolved. Boil for 5 minutes. Let cool, then pour over the vegetables and lemon. Cover and refrigerate for at least 24 hours or until needed. Keeps for 1 month in the refrigerator.

pickled ginger

150 g/5 oz. piece fresh ginger

1 tablespoon salt

125 ml/½ cup rice vinegar

115 g/½ cup plus 1 tablespoon
sugar

1 slice fresh beetroot/beet,
1 red radish, sliced, or a drop
of red food colouring (optional)

makes about 250 ml/1 cup

The subtle flavouring of raw fish, delicate rice and fresh vegetables can easily be overpowered by the lingering flavours of previous morsels, and so ginger helps cleanse the palate.

Peel the ginger and slice it very finely with a mandoline or vegetable peeler. Put it in a large sieve or colander and sprinkle over the salt. Set aside for 30 minutes, then rinse thoroughly.

Put the rice vinegar and sugar in a saucepan, add 60 ml/¼ cup water and bring to the boil, stirring until the sugar has dissolved. Boil for 5 minutes. Let cool, then pour over the ginger. If you would like it to be pink, like shop-bought ginger, add the beetroot, radish or food colouring. Cover and refrigerate for at least 24 hours or until needed.

wasabi paste

Most of the wasabi we buy in tubes is a mixture of horseradish and wasabi – or it can be just horseradish dyed green. If you buy wasabi paste from a Japanese market, you will have a selection of various qualities, and it is always preferable to buy the best. Many Japanese cooks prefer to mix their own wasabi paste from silver-grey wasabi powder, sold in small cans, believing that the flavour is stronger and sharper. The fresh roots are not widely available, even in Japan, but if you see them in a specialist greengrocer, sold on a bed of ice, do try them. To experience the real flavour and rush of wasabi you can make your own paste from them. Traditionally grated using a sharkskin grater, a porcelain ginger grater or a very fine abrasive zester will also work. After grating, the heat in wasabi lasts for only about 10 minutes, so you must use it straight away.

wasabi from powder
1 teaspoon wasabi powder

serves 1

fresh wasabi paste
1 fresh wasabi root

a wasabi grater or ginger grater

serves 6–8

wasabi from powder

Put the wasabi powder in a small bowl, such as an eggcup. Add 1 teaspoon water and mix with the end of a chopstick. Serve immediately.

fresh wasabi paste

Scrape or peel off the rough skin from the root. Using a circular motion, rub the wasabi gently against an abrasive grater onto a chopping board. Pound and chop the grated wasabi to a fine paste with a large knife or cleaver. Consume within 10 minutes.

Note To keep the wasabi from discolouring for as long as possible, turn the little bowl upside down until serving – this will stop the air getting at it.

2 maki

simple rolled sushi

Wonderful party food, nori rolls (*norimaki*) are probably the best-known sushi of all. A sheet of nori seaweed is spread with sushi rice, a line of filling put down the middle, then the sheet is rolled up into a cylinder. The cylinder is cut into sections before serving. All ingredients are available in Asian shops or larger supermarkets, as well as from online retailers.

18-cm/7-inch piece unwaxed cucumber, unpeeled

3 sheets of nori seaweed

¾ recipe vinegared rice (see page 13)

wasabi paste or powder

to serve

pickled ginger (see page 17)

extra wasabi paste

Japanese soy sauce (shoyu)

a sushi rolling mat

makes 36 pieces

To prepare the cucumber, cut into quarters lengthways, then cut out the seeds and cut the remainder, lengthways, into 1-cm/½-inch square matchstick lengths. You need 6 strips, each with some green skin.

Just before assembling, pass the nori over a very low gas flame or hotplate, just for a few seconds to make it crisp and bring out the flavour. Cut each sheet in half crossways.

Assemble the sushi according to the method on the following pages.

Cut each roll into 6 pieces, as shown on page 25.

Arrange on a serving plate and serve with pickled ginger, a little pile of wasabi paste and a dish of Japanese soy sauce.

step-by-step making simple rolls

Following on from the instructions on pages 22–23, make the vinegared rice (*sumeshi*), prepare and assemble the ingredients, then dip your hands in the bowl of hand vinegar.

1 Put a sushi rolling mat (*makisu*) on your work surface, then put half a sheet of toasted nori seaweed on top. Take a handful of the rice (2–3 heaped tablespoons) in your hands and make into a log shape. Put the rice in the centre of the nori.

2 Using your fingers, spread it evenly all over, leaving about 1.5-cm/½-inch margin on the far side. (The rice will stick to your hands, so have a bowl of hand vinegar – see page 26 – at the ready to dip them in as necessary.)

3 Take a small dot of wasabi paste on the end of your finger and draw a line down the middle across the rice, leaving a light green shadow on top of the rice (not too much – wasabi is very hot!).

4 Arrange 1 strip of cucumber across the rice, on top of the wasabi.

5 Pick up the mat from the near side and keep the cucumber in the centre.

4

5

6

6 Roll the mat over to meet the other side so that the rice stays inside the nori.

7 Lift the top edge of the mat. Press and roll the cylinder slightly. The join should be underneath so it will stick well (it sticks together because of the moisture in the rice). Remove the cylinder from the mat and put, join side down, in a covered flat container while you make the remaining rolls.

8 Cut each roll in half, then each half into 3, making 6 pieces. Arrange on a serving plate and serve with pickled ginger, a little pile of wasabi paste and a dish of Japanese soy sauce.

7

8

rolled sushi variations

¾ recipe vinegared rice
(see page 13), divided into
3 portions

3 sheets of nori seaweed

hand vinegar

4 tablespoons Japanese
rice vinegar

250 ml/1 cup water

fillings: your choice of

100 g/4 oz. fresh salmon,
skinned

6 cm/2½ inches pickled daikon
(takuan), cut lengthways into
1 cm/½-inch matchsticks

4–6 fresh shiso leaves or
6–8 basil leaves

2 small red pickled plums
(umeboshi), pitted/stoned and
torn into pieces

wasabi paste

to serve

pickled ginger (see page 17)

extra wasabi paste

Japanese soy sauce (shoyu)

a sushi rolling mat

makes 36 pieces

Other ingredients traditionally used for rolled sushi in Japan include *kanpyo* (dried gourd ribbons), tuna with spring onion, *natto* (steamed fermented soy beans), chilli-marinated cod's roe and *umeboshi* (salted plum) with shiso herb. You can also make variations using ingredients more readily available in the West.

Mix the hand vinegar ingredients in a small bowl and set aside.

Cut the piece of salmon into 1 cm/½ inch square strips. To make a salmon sushi, follow the method on pages 24–25, using a row of salmon strips instead of cucumber. (Enough to make 2 rolls.)

To make a pickled daikon sushi, follow the method on pages 24–25, using 3 strips of pickled daikon in a row instead of cucumber, and omitting the wasabi paste. (Enough to make 2 rolls.)

To make the pickled plum sushi, follow the method on pages 24–25, using the shiso or basil leaves and the pieces of plum. (Enough to make 2 rolls.)

Cut each roll into 6 pieces, then arrange on a plate and serve with pickled ginger, a mound of wasabi paste and a dish of soy sauce.

Note You can also leave the salmon fillet whole, then lightly grill/broil it for about 2 minutes on each side. Cool, put in a bowl, flake with a fork, then stir in 2 finely chopped spring onions/scallions. Mix in salt, pepper and 2 teaspoons mayonnaise, then proceed as in the main recipe.

big sushi rolls

A super-sized maki roll, known as *futomaki* in Japanese.

3 sheets of nori seaweed

1 recipe vinegared rice
(see page 13), divided into
6 portions

hand vinegar

4 tablespoons Japanese
rice vinegar

250 ml/1 cup water

fillings

9–12 uncooked king prawn/
jumbo shrimp tails, unpeeled

1 recipe Japanese omelette
(see page 14)

250 g/8 oz. spinach

3 tablespoons Japanese soy
sauce (shoyu)

20 g/1 oz. dried gourd
(*kanpyo*) or 1 carrot, cut into
5-mm/⅛-inch square shreds

5–6 dried shiitake mushrooms

2 tablespoons sugar

1 tablespoon mirin (sweetened
Japanese rice wine)
or sweet sherry

sea salt

to serve

Japanese soy sauce (shoyu)

pickled ginger (see page 17)

*8 cocktail sticks/toothpicks
or bamboo skewers*

a sushi rolling mat

makes 24 pieces

Mix the hand vinegar ingredients in a small bowl and set aside.

Skewer a cocktail stick through each prawn from head to tail to prevent curling while cooking. Blanch in boiling water for 3 minutes until firm and pink. Immediately plunge into cold water and drain. Remove and discard the cocktail sticks, shells and dark back vein.

Cut the Japanese omelette lengthways into 1-cm/½-inch square sticks.

Blanch the spinach in lightly salted water for 1 minute. Plunge into cold water. Drain and pat dry with kitchen paper. Sprinkle with 2 teaspoons soy sauce and set aside.

If using dried gourd, rub with salt and a little water, then soak in water for 10 minutes. Drain, then cut into 20-cm/8-inch lengths. Soak the shiitakes in warm water for 30 minutes, then drain, retaining the soaking water. Cut into 5-cm/2-inch strips. Put 250 ml/1 cup of the soaking liquid in a small saucepan with the remaining soy sauce, sugar and mirin. Bring to the boil. Add the gourd and shiitakes. Simmer over low heat for 15 minutes. Let cool in the liquid.

Toast the nori over a low gas flame or hotplate and put it crossways on a sushi rolling mat, following the method on pages 24–25. Dip your hands in the hand vinegar. Take 1 portion of rice and squeeze it between your hands into a firm ball. Put the rice ball on one side of the nori sheet in the middle and, using wet fingers, spread it evenly over the half side of nori, leaving about 3 cm/1 inch margin on the far side. Repeat this once more to fill the other half. The rice layer should be fairly thick – add extra rice if necessary.

Arrange 3–4 prawns in a row across the rice about 5 cm/2 inches from the front edge. Add a row of omelette strips and a row of spinach on top. Add a row of gourd and a row of shiitakes, so that all 5 ingredients are piled down the middle. Each roll should use one-third of each ingredient.

Pick up the mat from the near side and roll the mat following the method on page 25. Remove the mat and put the roll on a plate, join side down. Repeat to make 2 more rolls. Cut each roll into 8 pieces and serve with soy sauce and pickled ginger.

children's favourites

Sushi is fun when you make it for or with children. Devising sushi for non-Japanese kids has led to some surprise discoveries.

3 sheets of nori seaweed

¾ recipe vinegared rice (see page 13), divided into 6 portions

Japanese soy sauce (shoyu), to serve

hand vinegar

4 tablespoons Japanese rice vinegar

250 ml/1 cup water

fillings

1 egg, beaten

2 tablespoons sugar

6 cm/2½ inches carrot, sliced lengthways into 5-mm/⅛-inch matchsticks

2 thin frankfurters, 18 cm/ 7 inches long, or 4 Vienna sausages, 9 cm/4 inches long

6 cm/2½ inches unwaxed cucumber

75 g/3 oz. canned red salmon, drained

1 tablespoon mayonnaise

sea salt

sunflower oil, for frying

a Japanese omelette pan or 20-cm/8-inch non-stick frying pan/skillet

a sushi rolling mat

makes 36 pieces

Mix the hand vinegar ingredients in a bowl and set aside.

To make the fillings, strain the egg into a small bowl, add ½ tablespoon of the sugar and a pinch of salt and beat until dissolved. Heat a frying pan, brush with oil, then rub off any excess with kitchen paper.

Pour in the egg mixture and make a thin pancake, tilting the pan to spread it evenly. Prick any bubbles with a fork and fill any holes with egg by tilting the pan. After 30 seconds, turn the omelette over for 30 seconds to dry the other side and make it golden yellow. Remove from the heat, remove with a spatula and cut in half.

Blanch the carrot in 250 ml/1 cup boiling salted water for 2–3 minutes. Reduce the heat, then stir in the remaining 1½ tablespoons sugar and a pinch of salt. Simmer gently for 2–3 minutes, remove from the heat and let cool in the juice.

Put half the omelette on a board with the cut side nearest you and put a row of carrot strips beside the cut edge. Roll up the omelette tightly and secure the end with a cocktail stick. Repeat to make a second roll.

Cook the sausages according to the packet instructions and drain well on kitchen paper. Cut into 1-cm/½-inch square matchsticks. Thickly peel the cucumber and finely shred the skin.

Put the canned salmon in a bowl, add the mayonnaise and pinch of salt and stir well.

Following the method on pages 24–25, make 2 sushi rolls with a carrot-and-egg-roll filling (remove the cocktail sticks first), 2 rolls with strips of sausage and 2 with salmon paste and cucumber.

Cut each roll into 6 pieces and serve with soy sauce.

spicy tuna roll

Fresh tuna is one of the most popular fillings for sushi. There are three main cuts, the pink *otoro* (the finest), *chutoro* and the dark red *akami*. With their incredible popularity and high price tags, *otoro* and *chutoro* are delicacies reserved for sashimi, but the *akami* is perfect for rolled sushi.

300 g/10 oz. fresh tuna

2 tablespoons Japanese soy sauce (shoyu)

1 tablespoon sake

1 teaspoon Chinese hot pepper sauce, or chilli/chili sauce

2 spring onions/scallions, finely chopped

3 sheets of nori seaweed, halved

½ recipe vinegared rice (see page 13), divided into 6 portions

hand vinegar

4 tablespoons Japanese rice vinegar

250 ml/1 cup water

a sushi rolling mat

makes 36–42 pieces

Mix the hand vinegar ingredients in a small bowl and set aside.

Slice the tuna into 1 cm/½-inch strips and put in a shallow dish. Mix the soy sauce, sake, hot pepper sauce and spring onions in a bowl. Pour over the tuna and stir well to coat. Cover and let marinate for 30 minutes. Divide into 6 portions.

Put ½ sheet of nori, rough side up with the long edge towards you, on a sushi rolling mat. Dip your fingers in the hand vinegar, then top the nori with 1 portion of vinegared rice and spread in a thin layer, leaving about 2 cm/¾ inch of bare nori on the far edge. Set 1 portion of the tuna strips in a line along the middle of the rice.

Lift the near edge of the mat and start rolling the sushi away from you, pressing in the filling with your fingers as you roll. You may need a little water along the far edge to seal it. Repeat to make 6 rolls. Using a clean wet knife, slice each roll into 6–7 even pieces.

wasabi mayonnaise & tuna roll

This is a rather Western idea of sushi, but it is easy and convenient because it uses canned tuna, cutting out some of the fiddly preparation of fresh fish. Use Japanese mayonnaise if you can, but homemade or good-quality shop-bought mayonnaise works well.

4 sheets of nori seaweed

185 g/6½ oz. canned tuna in brine, drained

4 teaspoons Japanese or other mayonnaise

1 teaspoon wasabi paste, or to taste

125 g/4½ oz. baby corn, fresh or frozen, or equivalent drained canned baby corn

½ recipe vinegared rice (see page 13), divided into 4 portions

a sushi rolling mat

makes 24–28 pieces

Trim a 2.5 cm/1-inch strip from one long edge of each sheet of nori and reserve for another use.

Put the tuna and mayonnaise in a bowl and stir in the wasabi.

If using fresh or frozen corn, bring a saucepan of water to the boil and cook the corn for 3 minutes, or until tender. Drain and rinse under cold water to cool. If using canned corn, drain and rinse.

Set a sheet of nori, rough side up, on a rolling mat with the long edge towards you. Top with 1 portion of the sushi rice, and spread it in a thin layer, leaving about 2 cm/¾ inch of bare nori on the far edge. Spoon a quarter of the tuna mixture in a line along the middle of the rice and top with a line of corn, set end to end.

Lift the edge of the mat closest to you and start rolling up the sushi away from you, pressing in the filling with your fingers as you roll. You may need a little water along the far edge to seal it. Repeat to make 4 rolls. Using a clean, wet knife, slice each roll into 6–7 even pieces.

vinegared mackerel & avocado maki roll

Soaking in vinegar is a way of mellowing the strong flavours of some fish, such as mackerel. If you don't have time to prepare fresh mackerel, try making this sushi with smoked mackerel or other smoked fish for a different, but still delicious flavour.

400 g/1 lb. fresh mackerel fillets (about 2 medium fillets)

2 tablespoons sea salt

5 tablespoons rice vinegar

1 tablespoon sugar

1 avocado

3 sheets of nori seaweed, halved

½ recipe vinegared rice (see page 13), divided into 6 portions

1 teaspoon wasabi paste (optional)

hand vinegar

4 tablespoons Japanese rice vinegar

250 ml/1 cup water

a sushi rolling mat

makes 36–42 pieces

Mix the hand vinegar ingredients in a small bowl and set aside.

Put the mackerel fillets in a shallow, non-metallic bowl and sprinkle on both sides with the salt. Cover with clingfilm/plastic wrap and refrigerate for 8 hours or overnight.

Remove the fish from the refrigerator, rinse under cold running water and pat dry with kitchen paper. Put the vinegar and sugar in a shallow dish, mix well, then add the mackerel, turning to coat. Let marinate for 40 minutes at room temperature.

Remove the fish from the marinade and slice diagonally into 1-cm/½-inch strips. Slice the avocado into 1-cm/½-inch strips.

Put a sheet of nori, rough side up with the long edge towards you, on a sushi rolling mat. Dip your fingers in the hand vinegar, take 1 portion of the vinegared rice and spread it out in a thin layer, leaving about 2 cm/¾ inch bare on the far edge. Smear a little wasabi, if using, down the middle of the rice. Arrange a line of mackerel slices over the wasabi and top with a line of the avocado.

Lift the near edge of the mat and start rolling the sushi away from you, pressing in the filling with your fingers as you roll. You may need a little water along the far edge to seal it. Repeat with the remaining ingredients to make 6 rolls. Using a clean, wet knife, slice each roll into 6–7 even pieces of sushi.

fresh oyster roll with chilli cucumber

A fresh oyster makes such an elegantly simple topping for sushi. Chose small oysters if possible – large ones will swamp a delicate roll.

2 sheets of nori seaweed

½ recipe vinegared rice (see page 13), divided into 2 portions

freshly squeezed juice of 1 lemon

20 small raw oysters, shucked

chilli cucumber

125 ml/½ cup white rice vinegar

2 tablespoons sugar

1 tablespoon mirin (sweetened Japanese rice wine)

7-cm/3-inch piece cucumber, halved, deseeded and cut into fine matchsticks

2 mild red chillies/chiles, halved, deseeded and finely sliced

hand vinegar

4 tablespoons Japanese rice vinegar

250 ml/1 cup water

a sushi rolling mat

makes 20 pieces

To make the chilli cucumber, put the vinegar, sugar and mirin in a small saucepan and bring to the boil, stirring. Reduce the heat and simmer for 3 minutes. Remove from the heat and let cool.

Put the cucumber and chillies in a plastic bowl and pour over the cooled vinegar mixture. Cover and refrigerate for 24 hours.

When ready to assemble the rolls, mix the hand vinegar ingredients in a small bowl and set aside.

Put a sheet of nori, rough side up with the long edge towards you, on a sushi rolling mat. Dip your fingers in the hand vinegar, take 1 portion of the vinegared rice and spread it out in a thin layer, leaving about 2 cm/¾ inch bare on the far edge. Lift the edge of the mat closest to you and start rolling the sushi away from you. You may need a little water along the far edge to seal it. Press the roll into an oval. Repeat with the remaining ingredients to make a second roll.

Using a clean, wet knife, slice each roll in half, then each half into 5 even pieces, making 20.

Sprinkle lemon juice over the oysters. Top each piece of sushi with an oyster and a little chilli cucumber.

yakitori octopus roll

Yakitori is the name given to food grilled on skewers over a charcoal fire. It can be anything – chicken, steak, liver or the octopus used here. Prawns/shrimp, scallops or any firm fish also work well. You should cook the octopus very fast over a fire to get an authentic flavour, but a hot grill/broiler will also work.

6 octopus tentacles, about 1 kg/2 lbs., tenderized, skin and suckers removed

6 spring onions/scallions

2 tablespoons sake

2 tablespoons Japanese soy sauce (shoyu)

1 teaspoon sugar

1 teaspoon freshly grated ginger

3 sheets of nori seaweed, halved

½ recipe vinegared rice (see page 13), divided into 6 portions

5 bamboo skewers, soaked in water for 30 minutes

a sushi rolling mat

makes 30 pieces

Cut the octopus into 2.5-cm/1-inch pieces. Cut the spring onions into 2.5-cm/1-inch lengths. Thread the pieces of octopus and spring onion alternately crossways onto the soaked skewers.

Put the sake, soy, sugar and ginger into a small bowl or jug/pitcher, mix well, then pour over the octopus skewers and let marinate at room temperature for 30 minutes, turning occasionally.

Preheat a barbecue or grill/broiler to very hot. Set the yakitori skewers about 7 cm/3 inches from the heat and cook for 4–5 minutes, turning once. Remove from the heat and let cool.

Put a sheet of nori, rough side up, on a rolling mat with the long edge towards you. Top with 1 portion of the sushi rice, spread in a thin layer, leaving about 2 cm/¾ inch of bare nori on the far edge. Arrange pieces of the octopus, end to end, in a line along the middle of the rice, then put a line of spring onions/scallions on top.

Lift the edge of the mat closest to you and start rolling up the sushi away from you, pressing in the filling with your fingers as you roll. You may need a little water along the far edge to seal it. Repeat to make 6 rolls. Using a clean wet knife, slice each roll into 5 even pieces.

Note If the octopus has not been pre-tenderized, you can either beat it with a meat mallet or try this Portuguese method. Wash well and put in a large saucepan with 1 sliced onion. Cover with a lid and slowly bring to the boil over low heat (there will be enough moisture in the octopus to do this without added water). Let simmer for 30–40 minutes until tender. Cool, then pull off and discard the purple skin and suckers.

pickled salmon roll

To many sushi fans, delicious raw fish is part of the pleasure of this dish. However, if you're not an aficionado of fish *au naturel*, using smoked or pickled fish is a delicious compromise. It is very easy to pickle fish at home, and you can control the sharpness more easily.

3 sheets of nori seaweed, halved

½ recipe vinegared rice (see page 13), divided into 6 portions

1 teaspoon wasabi paste (optional)

pickled salmon

100 ml/⅔ cup rice wine vinegar

2 teaspoons salt

2 tablespoons sugar

grated zest of 1 unwaxed lemon

300 g/10½ oz. salmon fillet, skinned and boned

4 shallots, finely sliced

a sushi rolling mat

makes 36–42 pieces

To prepare the salmon, put the vinegar, salt, sugar and lemon zest in a saucepan with 60 ml/¼ cup water. Bring to the boil, reduce the heat, then simmer for 3 minutes. Let cool.

Put the salmon fillet in a plastic container with the shallots. Pour the vinegar mixture over the top and cover tightly. Refrigerate for 2–3 days, turning the salmon in the pickle once a day.

When ready to make the sushi, drain the salmon and shallots. Slice the salmon as finely as possible and divide into 6 portions.

Put a half sheet of nori, rough side up, on a rolling mat with the long edge towards you. Top with 1 portion of the sushi rice and spread it out in a thin layer, leaving about 2 cm/¾ inch of bare nori at the far edge. Smear a little wasabi paste down the centre of the rice if you like. Arrange 1 portion of the salmon slices in a line along the middle of the rice and top with a line of the pickled shallots.

Lift the edge of the mat closest to you and start rolling the sushi away from you, pressing in the filling with your fingers as you roll. You may need a little water along the far edge to seal it. Repeat with the remaining ingredients to make 6 rolls. Using a clean wet knife, slice each roll into 6–7 even pieces.

tempura prawn roll

The crunch of tempura batter is delicious in sushi, although the batter will soften as it cools. If you have some left over, use it to cook vegetables for a fantastic appetizer.

24 large uncooked prawns/jumbo shrimp, peeled, but with tail fins intact

2 sheets of nori seaweed

½ recipe vinegared rice (see page 13)

1 teaspoon wasabi (optional)

25 g/1 oz. mizuna or baby spinach

peanut or sunflower/safflower oil, for frying

tempura batter

1 egg, separated

1 tablespoon freshly squeezed lemon juice

150 ml/⅔ cup iced water

60 g/scant ⅓ cup plain/all-purpose flour

hand vinegar

4 tablespoons Japanese rice vinegar

250 ml/1 cup water

24 bamboo skewers

makes 24 pieces

Fill a large wok or saucepan one-third full with oil and heat to 190°C (375°F), or until a small cube of bread turns golden in 30 seconds.

Thread each prawn onto a skewer to straighten it for cooking.

To make the batter, put the egg yolk, lemon juice and iced water in a bowl. Whisk gently, then whisk in the flour to form a smooth batter. Do not overmix.

Whisk the egg white in a second bowl until stiff but not dry, then fold into the batter.

Dip each prawn into the batter and fry for 1–2 minutes until crisp and golden. Drain on crumpled kitchen paper and let cool for 5 minutes. Remove the skewers.

Mix the hand vinegar ingredients in a small bowl and set aside.

Using dry hands, cut the nori sheets in half crossways and then into 3 cm/1-inch strips. Spread 1 tablespoon of rice over each piece of nori, top with a tempura prawn, a dab of wasabi, if using, and a little mizuna or baby spinach. Roll up to secure the filling. Brush the nori with water to help it stick, if necessary. Repeat until all the ingredients have been used.

battleship sushi

Strictly speaking battleship sushi are more of a nigiri sushi as they are individually hand rolled, but as the nori still appears on the outside of the sushi, they still feel at home in this chapter. After the rice is shaped, the nori is wrapped around it so that it comes about a ½ cm/¼ inch above the rice, leaving room for less manageable toppings such as fish roe. Small cubes of different-coloured fish make a lovely topping and you don't need to be an expert fish slicer to get tender pieces. You do, however, need very fresh raw fish – that is what 'sushi- or sashimi-grade' means. If you have access to a proper Japanese fishmonger, that's perfect. Otherwise, go to a fish market, or other outlet where you can be sure the fish is ultra-fresh.

75 g/3 oz. piece of sushi-grade raw salmon

75 g/3 oz. piece of sushi-grade raw tuna

75 g/3 oz. piece of sushi-grade raw white fish (try sea bream or halibut)

½ recipe vinegared rice (see page 13)

4 sheets of nori seaweed

1 teaspoon wasabi paste (optional)

1 tablespoon salmon caviar (keta)

a sushi rolling mat

makes 18 pieces

Cut the salmon, tuna and white fish into ½-cm/¼-inch cubes, put in a bowl and mix gently.

Divide the seasoned sushi rice into 18 portions, a little smaller than a table tennis ball. Gently squeeze each piece into a flattened oval shape, about 2 cm/¾ inch high. With dry hands, cut the nori sheets into 2.5-cm/1-inch strips, and wrap each piece of rice in one strip with the rough side of the nori facing inwards. Seal the ends with a dab of water. You should have about ½ cm/¼ inch of nori above the rice.

Put a dab of wasabi, if using, on top of the rice, then add a heaped teaspoon of the fish cubes, and a little salmon caviar.

treasures of the sea sushi

This battleship-shaped sushi has a ribbon of nori seaweed wrapped vertically around the rice, with added toppings such as salmon caviar (*ikura* or *keta*) and sea urchin. This recipe includes Western variations using crabmeat.

1½ sheets of nori seaweed

½ recipe vinegared rice (see page 13)

hand vinegar

4 tablespoons Japanese rice vinegar

250 ml/1 cup water

toppings

8–12 tablespoons crabmeat*

about 1 teaspoon sake

2 teaspoons wasabi paste or powder

4–6 tablespoons salmon caviar (*ikura* or *keta*) or red lumpfish caviar

12 pickled caperberries or capers

to serve

pickled ginger (see page 17)

Japanese soy sauce (shoyu)

makes 12 pieces

*Use white and brown crabmeat from your fishmonger, or good-quality canned crab.

Mix the hand vinegar ingredients in a small bowl and set aside.

Put the crabmeat on a small plate and sprinkle with a little sake. If using wasabi powder, mix 1–2 teaspoons powder in an egg cup along with 1–2 teaspoons water to make a clay-like consistency. Turn it upside down and set aside to prevent it drying.

Cut the whole sheet of nori crossways into 8 ribbons, 18 x 2.5 cm/ 7 x 1 inches, and the ½ sheet into 4, making 12 ribbons in total.

Dip your hands in the hand vinegar, then take 1–2 tablespoons rice in one hand and squeeze it into a rectangular mound about 5 x 2 x 3 cm/ 2 x ¾ x 1¼ inches high. Wrap a nori ribbon around it, overlapping about 2 cm/¾ inch at the end. Glue it together with a grain of vinegared rice. Put 2 teaspoons caviar and a few pickled caperberries or capers on top. Repeat to make 3 more rolls with caviar, 4 with crabmeat topped with a little salmon caviar and 4 with crabmeat, with a tiny dot of wasabi on top.

Arrange on a platter, then serve with the pickled ginger and a small dish of soy sauce as party food. If making individual servings, serve the soy sauce in small, separate dishes.

teriyaki chicken roll with miso dipping sauce

Fragrant teriyaki chicken is wonderful served on its own, but can also act as the perfect filling for sushi rolls. You can buy pre-prepared teriyaki sauces or marinades, but it is well worth taking the extra time to make your own.

400 g/14 oz. boneless, skinless chicken thigh or breast (2 breasts, 4 thighs), cut into 1-cm/½-inch strips

4 sheets of nori seaweed

½ recipe vinegared rice (see page 13), divided into 4 portions

1 teaspoon wasabi paste

teriyaki sauce

2 tablespoons Japanese soy sauce (shoyu)

2 tablespoons mirin (sweetened Japanese rice wine)

2 tablespoons chicken stock

teriyaki glaze

1 teaspoon sugar

½ teaspoon cornflour/ cornstarch

miso dipping sauce

2 tablespoons white miso paste

1 tablespoon sugar

125 ml/½ cup sake

1 small egg yolk

12 bamboo skewers, soaked in water for 30 minutes

a sushi rolling mat

makes 24–28 pieces

To make the teriyaki sauce, mix the soy, mirin and chicken stock in a small saucepan and bring to the boil. Remove from the heat and let cool.

To make the teriyaki glaze, mix the sugar and cornflour/cornstarch in a small bowl with a little cold water to slacken, then stir in 2 tablespoons of the teriyaki sauce. Set aside.

Thread the strips of chicken onto the soaked skewers. Brush the chicken skewers with half the teriyaki sauce and let marinate for about 10 minutes. Preheat a grill/broiler or barbecue to very hot. Set the chicken skewers under the grill. Grill/broil for 2–3 minutes, turn the skewers over and brush with more sauce and grill for a further 2–3 minutes until cooked. Remove from the heat, pour over the teriyaki glaze, let cool, then unthread. The chicken must be cold.

Set a sheet of nori, rough side up, on a rolling mat with the long edge towards you. Top with quarter of the sushi rice, spread in a thin layer covering about half of the nori closest to you. Put a quarter of the chicken in a line along the middle of the rice and smear with a little wasabi.

Lift the edge of the mat closest to you and start rolling up the sushi away from you, pressing in the filling with your fingers as you roll. You may need a little water along the far edge to seal it. Repeat with the remaining ingredients, to make 4 rolls. Using a clean wet knife, slice each roll into 6–7 even pieces.

To make the white miso dipping sauce, put the miso, sugar and sake in a small saucepan over medium heat and bring to a simmer, reduce the heat to low, and cook for 3 minutes, stirring constantly to stop it burning.

Remove from the heat and quickly stir in the egg yolk, strain if necessary, and let cool before serving with the sushi.

five-colour roll

Futo-maki (thick rolled) sushi are great for lunch, because they are more substantial than *hosi-maki* (thin rolled). However, they aren't ideal for fingerfood, because they are more than one mouthful.

10 g/½ oz. dry gourd*

2 teaspoons salt, for rubbing

250 ml/1 cup dashi or fish stock

2 teaspoons Japanese soy sauce (shoyu)

2 teaspoons mirin (sweetened Japanese rice wine)

1 teaspoon sugar

3 large eggs

a pinch of salt

2 teaspoons peanut oil

150 g/1½ cups spinach leaves, washed

3 sheets of nori seaweed

½ recipe vinegared rice (see page 13)

1 small red (bell) pepper, halved, deseeded and cut into fine strips

1 carrot, grated or very thinly sliced

a 28-cm/12-inch frying pan/skillet

a sushi rolling mat

makes 24 pieces

*Gourd (kampyo or calabash) is sold dried in Japanese shops. It is a common ingredient in rolled sushi, and worth trying.

Fill a bowl with water, add the dried gourd, rub the salt into the gourd to wash it, then drain and rinse thoroughly. Cover the gourd with fresh water and soak for 1 hour. Drain, then put in a saucepan, cover with boiling water and cook for 5 minutes. Drain, return to the pan, then add the dashi, 1 teaspoon of the soy, 1 teaspoon of the mirin and the sugar. Bring to the boil, reduce the heat and simmer for 5 minutes. Let cool in the liquid, then drain.

Put the eggs in a bowl, add the salt and remaining soy and mirin, and mix well. Heat the oil in the frying pan over medium heat. Pour in the eggs, swirling the pan so the mixture covers the base. Cook for 2–3 minutes, gently gathering in the cooked omelette around the edges to let the uncooked egg run onto the hot pan. When the egg is set, take off the heat and fold in the 4 sides, so they meet in the middle and the omelette is now double thickness and square. Remove to a board, let cool, then slice into 3 strips.

Wipe out and reheat the pan. Add the washed but still wet spinach and cover. Cook for 1½–2 minutes until wilted. Tip into a colander and let cool for a few minutes. Using your hands, squeeze out the liquid from the wilted spinach.

Put 1 nori sheet on a rolling mat, rough side up, and spread with one-third of the rice, leaving 3 cm/1¼ inch nori bare at the far edge. Put a strip of omelette in the middle and put one-third of the gourd, spinach, pepper and carrot, laid in lengthways strips on top.

Carefully roll up the nori in the mat, pressing the ingredients into the roll as you go. Wet the bare edge of nori and finish rolling to seal. Repeat to make 3 rolls, then cut each one into 8 pieces.

smoked trout & wasabi sushi

This simple, traditional sushi uses smoked trout, which is a good alternative to smoked salmon. The contrast of fresh and crisp cucumber is a welcome addition.

1 sheet of nori seaweed

½ recipe vinegared rice (see page 13), divided into 2 portions

2 teaspoons wasabi paste (watered down with a little water if liked)

100 g/3½ oz. sliced smoked trout, cut into strips

1 mini cucumber, deseeded and sliced lengthways

hand vinegar

4 tablespoons Japanese rice vinegar

250 ml/1 cup water

to serve

Japanese soy sauce (shoyu)

pickled ginger (see page 17)

wasabi paste

a sushi rolling mat

makes 12 pieces

Mix the hand vinegar ingredients in a small bowl.

Toast the nori over a gas flame or hotplate and cut it in half. Put one piece on a sushi rolling mat.

Dip your hands in the hand vinegar and press each portion of rice into a cylinder shape. Put the cylinder on the piece of nori and spread it evenly over the sheet, leaving about 2 cm/¾ inch margin on the far side.

Brush 1 teaspoon wasabi down the middle of the rice and top with a line of smoked trout strips and a line of cucumber on top.

Roll it up following the method on pages 24–25, then make a second roll using the remaining ingredients.

The sushi can be wrapped in clingfilm/plastic wrap and left like this until you are ready to cut and serve.

To serve, cut in half with a wet knife and trim off the end (optional – you may like to leave a 'cockade' of cucumber sticking out the end). Cut each half in 3 and arrange on a serving platter. Serve with soy sauce, pickled ginger and wasabi paste.

bright vegetable & thin omelette rolls

3 large/extra-large eggs

2 teaspoons Japanese soy sauce (shoyu)

2–3 teaspoons peanut oil

3 sheets of nori seaweed, halved

½ recipe vinegared rice (see page 13), divided into 6 portions

100 g/4 oz. mixed vegetables (see recipe introduction), shredded into fine matchsticks

1 teaspoon wasabi paste (optional)

hand vinegar

4 tablespoons Japanese rice vinegar

250 ml/1 cup water

a Japanese omelette pan or 20-cm/8-inch frying pan/skillet

a sushi rolling mat

makes 36 pieces

This simple little roll makes a colourful addition to a sushi board. Try using a selection of different vegetables such as carrot, cucumber, radish, beetroot/beet, and red, yellow or orange (bell) peppers.

Mix the hand vinegar ingredients in a small bowl and set aside.

Put the eggs and soy sauce in a jug or bowl and beat well. Heat a film of oil in the pan and pour in one-third of the beaten egg mixture. Swirl the egg around to cover the base of the pan and cook for about 1 minute until set. Carefully remove the omelette to a plate and cook the remaining egg mixture in 2 batches. Cut each omelette in half.

Put a sheet of nori, rough side up with the long edge towards you, on a sushi rolling mat. Dip your hands in the hand vinegar and top the nori with 1 portion of the rice and piece of omelette (trim the end of the omelette if it hangs over the end of the rice). Arrange a line of vegetables along the edge closest to you and smear a little wasabi, if using, in a line next to the vegetables.

Carefully roll up, brushing a little water along the edge of the nori to seal if necessary. Repeat to make 6 rolls, then slice each roll into 6 even pieces.

miso-marinated asparagus roll

Using just one simple ingredient can make a perfectly elegant filling for rolled sushi. Here, fresh green asparagus is marinated in white miso.

24 small or 12 medium asparagus spears

100 g/4 oz. white miso paste

2 teaspoons mirin (sweetened Japanese rice wine)

1 teaspoon wasabi paste

3 sheets of nori seaweed, halved

½ recipe vinegared rice (see page 13), divided into 6 portions

a sushi rolling mat

makes 36 pieces

Snap off any tough ends of the asparagus and discard. Bring a large saucepan of water to the boil, add the asparagus spears and simmer for 3–4 minutes until tender. Drain, rinse in plenty of cold water, then let cool.

If using medium-sized asparagus spears, slice each piece in half lengthways to give 24 pieces in total. Arrange all the asparagus in a shallow dish.

Put the white miso paste, mirin and wasabi paste in a small bowl and mix well. Spread evenly over the asparagus and let marinate for 2–4 hours.

When ready to assemble the rolls, carefully scrape the marinade off the asparagus - it should be fairly clean so the miso doesn't overwhelm the flavour of the finished sushi.

Put 1 half-sheet of nori, rough side up, on the rolling mat. The long edge of the nori sheet should be towards you. Spread 1 portion in a thin layer over the nori, leaving about 2 cm/¾ inch bare on the far edge.

Put 4 pieces of the asparagus in a line along the middle of the rice. Lift the edge of the mat closest to you and start rolling up the sushi away from you, pressing in the filling with your fingers as you roll. You may need a little water along the far edge to seal it. Repeat to make 6 rolls in all.

Using a clean, wet knife, slice each roll into 6 even pieces and serve.

mushroom omelette sushi roll

Mushrooms are a very popular Japanese vegetable. Most supermarkets carry fresh shiitakes, and also may have enokis, which look like little clumps of white nails with tiny caps, and their bigger brothers, the hon-shigiri, with brown 'berets' on their heads. If unavailable, use oyster and button mushrooms.

100 g/4 oz. fresh shiitake mushrooms, about 12, stalks removed

100 g/4 oz. oyster mushrooms

50 g/2 oz. enoki mushrooms, roots trimmed

3 teaspoons peanut oil

1 tablespoon Japanese soy sauce (shoyu)

1 tablespoon mirin (sweetened Japanese rice wine)

2 eggs

¼ teaspoon salt

½ recipe vinegared rice (see page 13), divided into 4 portions

4 sheets of nori seaweed

a Japanese omelette pan or 23-cm/9-inch frying pan/skillet, preferably non-stick

a sushi rolling mat

makes 24–32 pieces

Slice the shiitake and oyster mushrooms into 1-cm/½-inch slices. Separate the enoki mushrooms into bunches of two or three.

Heat 2 teaspoons of the oil in a large frying pan/skillet and sauté the shiitake and oyster mushrooms for 2 minutes, add the enoki and stir-fry for 1½ minutes. Add the soy sauce and mirin and toss to coat. Remove from the heat and let cool. Divide into 4 portions.

Put the eggs and salt in a bowl and beat well. Heat ½ teaspoon of the oil in a frying pan. Slowly pour in half of the egg, tipping the pan to get an even coating. Cook for about 1 minute until set, roll up, remove from the pan and let cool. Repeat with the remaining egg to make a second omelette. Slice the two rolled omelettes in half lengthways.

Put 1 nori sheet on a rolling mat, rough side up, and spread with 1 portion of rice, leaving 3 cm/1¼ inch of bare nori at the far edge. Put a strip of omelette down the middle and top with 1 portion of the mushrooms. Carefully roll up the nori in the mat, pressing the ingredients into the roll as you go. Wet the bare edge of nori and finish rolling to seal. Repeat to make 4 rolls. Slice each roll into 6–8 pieces and serve.

honey soy mackerel & daikon maki

The combination of marinated mackerel with the crunch of daikon radish makes this a delicious party food bite.

½ recipe vinegared rice
(see page 13)

1½ sheets of nori seaweed

3 pea-sized drops of
wasabi paste

3 x 1-cm/½-inch strips pickled
daikon radish

1 fillet smoked honey soy
mackerel (approx 80 g/3 oz.)

a sushi rolling mat

makes 18–21 pieces

Fold the whole nori sheet in half across the grain and carefully tear in two. Lay the nori, shiny-side down, on a sushi mat.

Wet your hands slightly. Take one-third of the rice and spread it evenly over the nori. Leave 1 cm/½ inch free of rice along the top edge.

Gently press the rice down and spread a pea-sized drop of wasabi paste across the length of the rice. Line one strip of daikon along the middle of the rice and one-third of the mackerel next to it. Bring the bottom edge of the mat up and roll so that the top edge of the nori meets the edge of the rice. Apply gentle pressure so that the roll is tight and the margin of nori will overlap. Put the roll to one side with the overlap at the base. The moisture present in the rice will stick the nori together.

Repeat with the other 2 nori sheets and the remaining ingredients, keeping the finished roll covered. Slice each roll into 6 (or 7 if you like the look of filling coming out of the end, as **pictured overleaf, left**).

crabstick & avocado maki

Crab is a wonderful addition to this sushi, but you can replace it with cooked prawns/shrimp if you prefer.

½ recipe vinegared rice (see page 13)

1½ sheets of nori seaweed

3 pea-sized drops of wasabi paste

1 just-ripe avocado, halved and stone/pit removed

120 g/4 oz. good-quality crabsticks, sliced into thin strips (or cooked prawns/shrimp)

a sushi rolling mat

makes 18–21 pieces

Fold the whole nori sheet in half across the grain and carefully tear in two. Lay the nori, shiny-side down, on a sushi mat (or folded kitchen towel).

Wet your hands slightly. Take one-third of the rice and spread it evenly over the nori. Leave 1 cm/½ inch free of rice along the top edge.

Gently press the rice down and spread a pea-sized drop of wasabi paste across the length of the rice. Slice the avocado into thin strips. Line one-third of the avocado strips along the middle of the rice and one-third of the crabsticks next to it. Bring the bottom edge of the mat up and roll so that the top edge of the nori meets the edge of the rice. Apply gentle pressure so that the roll is tight and the margin of nori will overlap.

Put the roll to one side with the overlap at the base. The moisture present in the rice will stick the nori together.

Repeat with the other 2 nori sheets and the remaining ingredients, keeping the finished roll covered. Slice each roll into 6 (or 7 if you like the look of filling coming out of the end, as **pictured overleaf, right**).

smoked salmon & cucumber sushi rolls

This isn't so difficult to make – and very impressive. A smoked salmon fillet (sometimes known as royal fillet) is best used here. It is very meaty and you can cut it to the size you want. It may not be truly authentic, but it is great served with drinks on a hot summer's night. The uncut rolls can be wrapped up tightly in clingfilm/plastic wrap, then cut and unwrapped at the last moment to preserve the freshness.

1 recipe vinegared rice (see page 13), divided into 5 portions

1 large cucumber, unwaxed if possible

5 sheets of nori seaweed

200 g/8 oz. sliced smoked salmon

3 teaspoons wasabi paste

to serve

pickled ginger (see page 17)

Japanese soy sauce (shoyu)

wasabi paste

a sushi rolling mat or a clean cloth

makes 30 pieces

Cut the cucumber into strips the length of the long side of the nori.

To make the sushi rolls, put a sheet of nori shiny side down on a sushi mat or clean cloth. Spread one portion of the rice over the nori, leaving a clear strip down one long edge. Cover the rice with a thin layer of smoked salmon and spread with a little wasabi paste (thin it down with a little water if you like). Put a cucumber strip along the side opposite the clear strip of seaweed. Dampen the clear end. Starting from the cucumber end, and using the mat to help you, roll up like a Swiss roll, sealing it into a secure cylinder with the dampened edge.

Using a very sharp knife, cut into 2-cm/1-inch lengths. Repeat with the remaining seaweed, rice and salmon. Serve with pickled ginger, soy sauce and more wasabi for dipping.

3 uramaki

prawn uramaki

This prawn tempura version of uramaki is popular in restaurants – the nori prevents the vinegar in the rice and the oil in the tempura from touching each other.

2 sheets of nori seaweed

¾ recipe vinegared rice (see page 13), divided into 4 portions

hand vinegar

2 tablespoons Japanese rice vinegar

125 ml/½ cup water

tempura prawns

8 large uncooked tiger prawns/ jumbo shrimp, 4 peeled completely, 4 left with tail fins intact, deveined

100 g/⅔ cup plain/all-purpose flour, sifted

4 tablespoons sesame seeds, black or white

sea salt

sunflower oil, for frying

to serve

pickled ginger (see page 17)

Japanese soy sauce (shoyu)

8 cocktail sticks/toothpicks or bamboo skewers

a sushi rolling mat

makes 20 pieces

Mix the hand vinegar ingredients in a small bowl. Skewer a cocktail stick through each prawn from top to tail to prevent curling while cooking.

Cover one side of a sushi rolling mat with clingfilm/plastic wrap and put it on a dry cutting board, clingfilm side up.

Fill a wok or deep saucepan one-third full of oil and heat to 170°C (340°F) or until a cube of bread browns in 60 seconds. To make the tempura batter, put 100 ml/½ cup water in a bowl, sift the flour into the water and mix with a fork. One by one, dip the prawns in the batter, then fry in the hot oil for 3–4 minutes or until golden brown. Remove and drain on kitchen paper and carefully remove and discard the cocktail sticks.

Put the nori on a completely dry cutting board. Dip your hands in the hand vinegar. Take a handful of the rice (2–3 heaped tablespoons) in your hands and make into a log shape. Put the rice in the centre of the nori. Using your fingers, spread it evenly all over, right to the edges. Sprinkle 1 tablespoon sesame seeds all over the rice.

Turn the whole thing over onto the clingfilm-covered mat.

Arrange 2 tempura prawns down the centre of the nori, with the tails sticking out at the ends (remove the tail fins if you like).

Roll the mat following the method on pages 24–25. Remove from the mat and repeat to make 3 more rolls.

Cut each roll into 5 pieces and arrange on a platter. Serve with pickled ginger and a little soy sauce in a small dish beside the platter or in small individual plates.

inside-out avocado rolls with chives & cashews

2 small or 1 large ripe avocado

2 teaspoons freshly squeezed lemon juice

2 tablespoons Japanese mayonnaise

¼ teaspoon salt

1 teaspoon wasabi paste (optional)

75 g/3 oz. cashew nuts, pan-toasted (roasted, salted cashews work well)

a small bunch of chives

2 sheets of nori seaweed, halved

½ recipe vinegared rice (see page 13)

a sushi rolling mat

makes 24 pieces

Rolling inside-out sushi may seem a bit tricky, but it is actually very easy, because the rice on the outside moulds so well into shape, and it has the added bonus of looking spectacular.

Peel the avocado and cut the flesh into small chunks. Toss in a bowl with the lemon juice, mayonnaise, salt and wasabi, if using. Mash slightly as you toss but not until mushy. Divide into 4 portions.

Chop the cashew nuts very finely and put in a bowl. Chop the chives very finely and mix with the cashew nuts. Divide into 4 portions.

Put a sheet of clingfilm/plastic wrap on the rolling mat. Put half a sheet of nori on top, rough side up, with the long edge facing you. Divide the rice into 4 portions and spread 1 portion over the nori.

Sprinkle 1 portion of the nut and chive mixture on top of the rice. Press it in gently with your fingers.

Carefully lift the whole thing up and flip it over so the rice is face down on the clingfilm/plastic wrap. Remove the sushi mat. Put 1 portion of the avocado in a line along the long edge of the nori closest to you. Carefully roll it up, then cut in half, then cut each half into 3, giving 6 pieces. Repeat to make 4 rolls, giving 24 pieces.

smoked mackerel sushi rolls

Sushi is so quick and easy to make at home, with the added bonus of it being up to you what you fillings or flavourings you use so you can tailor it to your tastes.

5 sheets of nori seaweed

1 recipe vinegared rice (see page 13)

black sesame seeds, for sprinkling

350 g/12 oz. smoked mackerel, cut into thin strips

2 spring onions/scallions, cut into thin strips

½ red (bell) pepper, cut into thick strips

to serve

wasabi

picked ginger (see page 17)

light soy sauce

a sushi rolling mat

makes 30–40 pieces

Wrap the sushi mat in clingfilm/plastic wrap, squeezing out any trapped air. This helps prevent the rice from sticking. Lay the mat lengthways in front of you. Take one nori sheet and lay it out, shiny side down, on the bamboo mat. Wet your hands and take a small handful of rice. Starting at the far end, spread and pat the rice across the nori sheet leaving a bare, 1-cm/½-inch gap running along the edge of the sheet closest to you. You can add more rice if needed, but keep it even and no more than 1 cm/½ inch thick. If it starts sticking to your hands simply wet them again. You can also use the back of a spoon dipped in water.

Sprinkle black sesame seeds over the rice, then flip the nori sheet over so that the rice is now facing downward with the edge free of rice still closest to you and in line with the edge of the bamboo mat. Across the middle of the nori lay 3 lines of mackerel, spring onion and red pepper.

Then, using the mat, roll the edge of the nori sheet closest to you over the filling in the middle, tucking it over firmly so the filling is enclosed. When it looks like you are about to roll the mat into the sushi roll, pull the mat back and continue to roll, applying even pressure and tightening as you roll, using the mat to shape it. Once the roll has come together, carefully take it off the mat, lay the mat over it and press and smooth the roll, compressing it tightly and evening out the ends. The roll will actually be more of a rectangular shape when you have finished. With a sharp and wet knife, cut the roll in half and then each half into 3 or 4 even pieces.

Repeat this process with the remaining ingredients.

Arrange the rolls on a plate with a mound of wasabi and pickled ginger and the soy sauce in a dish on the side.

grilled tofu roll

Silken tofu makes a moist, tender filling for these delicious rolls – firm tofu can be a bit tough. To make silken tofu a little firmer, put it in a bowl and cover it with boiling water before you start making the sushi.

175 g/6 oz. silken tofu

2 tablespoons Japanese soy sauce (shoyu)

1 tablespoon mirin (sweetened Japanese rice wine)

1 teaspoon sugar

3 sheets of nori seaweed, halved (you need 5 pieces, so you will have ½ sheet left over)

1 tablespoon white sesame seeds, toasted in a dry frying pan

1 tablespoon black sesame seeds

1 tablespoon *oboro* (dried pink fish flakes)

½ recipe vinegared rice (see page 13)

1 teaspoon wasabi paste, plus extra to serve

a baking sheet, lined with baking parchment

a sushi rolling mat

makes 24–32 pieces

Cut the tofu into 1-cm/½-inch square strips and arrange in a shallow dish. Put the soy sauce, mirin and sugar in a small bowl or jug/pitcher and mix well. Pour the mixture evenly over the tofu and set aside to marinate for 10 minutes.

Preheat the grill/broiler. Place the tofu on the prepared baking sheet and grill/broil for 2 minutes. Turn the pieces over, brush with marinade and grill for a further 2 minutes. Set aside to cool.

Cut half a sheet of nori into tiny shreds (about 3 mm/1⁄16 inch), put in a small bowl and stir in the white and black sesame seeds and oboro.

Divide the rice into 4 portions.

Spread a sheet of clingfilm/plastic wrap on top of the rolling mat. Put half a sheet of nori on this and spread with 1 portion of rice. Sprinkle with a quarter of the seed mixture, and press lightly into the rice.

Carefully lift the whole thing up and flip it over so the rice is face down on the clingfilm/plastic wrap. Arrange slices of grilled tofu along the long edge of the nori closest to you, smear with a little wasabi paste and carefully roll up. Repeat to make 4 rolls, then slice each roll into 6–8 pieces.

Serve with extra wasabi and your choice of accompaniments.

mixed vegan sushi

This vegan recipe gives the option of making both uramaki and maki types of sushi to create an eye-catching platter.

for the spread

65 g/½ cup dry-roasted sunflower seeds (or use 4 tablespoons tahini)

3 teaspoons umeboshi paste

1 tablespoon dark sesame oil

for the sushi

2 medium pickled gherkins, cut lengthways into strips, or other pickled vegetables (sauerkraut, daikon, etc.)

1 long carrot, cut lengthways into thin sticks

4 long spring onion/scallion leaves, washed and drained

4 toasted nori sheets

475 g/2⅔ cups cooked brown rice

1 long carrot, cut lengthways into thin sticks

for the dipping sauce

2 tablespoons fresh ginger juice

2 teaspoons tamari

2 tablespoons dry-roasted sesame seeds

4 tablespoons water

extra pickles and wasabi paste, to serve

a sushi rolling mat

makes 32 pieces

Prepare the spread by blending the sunflower seeds in a blender into a powder/butter, and then adding the umeboshi and oil. The spread is very salty and not meant to be eaten on its own!

Prepare a bowl full of lukewarm water to wet your hands with while making the sushi. Place each nori sheet in turn on a sushi mat, shiny-side down. Wet your hands and spread 120 g/¾ cup of the cooked rice evenly over the nori, except the top side, where you'll want to leave a 1-cm/⅓-in. margin to make it easier to roll and seal.

To make the maki, spread a tablespoon of the spread across the middle of the roll. Place the gherkin strips, carrot sticks and spring onion leaves over the spread, making sure the layer is not thick, as this will make for an overly thick sushi.

Starting from the bottom, roll up the nori and tuck in the vegetables. Continue rolling and press tightly so that the rolled sushi stays sealed. Before serving, slice each sushi into 8 same-sized pieces. Repeat the whole process for the other 3 nori sheets, so you end up with 32 pieces of sushi.

To make uramaki, cover the sushi mat with a sheet of clingfilm/plastic wrap and place one nori sheet on top. Wet your hands and spread 120–150 g/¾–1 cup of the rice over the nori, distributing it evenly up to the edges. Carefully flip the nori so that the rice side goes on top of the clingfilm/plastic wrap on the mat. Spoon a tablespoon of the spread in a strip across the middle of the roll. Place the gherkin, carrot sticks and spring onion leaves over the spread. Starting at the edge while pressing it firmly, roll up the sushi mat and continue until you reach the end of the mat. Be careful not to wrap the clingfilm/plastic wrap inside! Squeeze the sushi inside the mat with your hands. Unwrap before serving, and slice each sushi into 8 same-sized pieces. Roll each of these pieces in toasted sesame seeds.

To make the sauce, mix the ginger juice, tamari and water. Dip a piece of sushi in it, then, before eating, coat it in some sesame seeds (but not for the uramaki, as they won't need it!)

4 nigiri

hand-moulded sushi

Hand-moulded or *nigiri-zushi* is the king of all sushi. Though it looks simple, it is actually the most difficult to make and is not usually made at home, even in Japan.

⅓ recipe vinegared rice
(see page 13)

toppings

2 uncooked tiger prawn/shrimp
tails

1 fillet fresh tuna or salmon,
about 100 g/4 oz., skinned

1 fillet fresh white-fleshed fish
such sea bream or sole, about
100 g/4 oz., skinned

100 g/4 oz. squid, cleaned
and skinned

2 eggs, beaten

2 tablespoons dashi stock

1 teaspoon mirin or
sweet sherry

1 teaspoon Japanese soy sauce
(shoyu), plus extra to serve

2 teaspoons wasabi paste
or powder

2 shiso leaves or basil leaves

a small sheet of nori seaweed,
cut into ½-cm/¼-inch strips

sea salt

pickled ginger (see page 17),
to serve

cocktail sticks/toothpicks

a sushi rolling mat

makes 8–10 pieces

Skewer a cocktail stick/toothpick through each prawn/shrimp from top to tail to prevent curling while cooking. Blanch in boiling water for 2 minutes until lightly cooked and pink. Drain and put under running water. Remove and discard the cocktail sticks/toothpicks, shells and back vein. Make a slit up the belly lengthways and open out.

Slice the tuna or salmon and sea bream into rectangular pieces that are about 7 x 3 x 1 cm/3 x 1¼ x ½ inch thick. Cut the squid into similar rectangular pieces, and make fine slits on one side of each piece to make the squid more tender.

Using the beaten eggs, chicken stock, mirin and soy sauce, make an omelette following the method on page XX. Put the rolled omelette on a sushi rolling mat and tightly roll into a flat rectangular shape. When cool, cut 2 rectangular pieces, 7 x 3 x 1 cm/3 x 1¼ x ½ inch thick.

If using wasabi powder, mix with 2 teaspoons water in an egg cup and stir well to make a clay-like consistency. Leave upside down to prevent drying.

Take a handful (about 1–2 tablespoons) of the cooked rice in one hand and mould into a rectangular cylinder about 5 x 2.5 x 2.5 cm/2 x 1 x 1 inches. (Dip your fingers in hand vinegar if the rice is sticking to them.) Put a tiny bit of wasabi on top and cover with an opened prawn/shrimp.

Repeat, making 2 nigiri topped with prawns/shrimp, 2 with tuna or salmon, 2 with sea bream, 2 with squid on top of a shiso leaf and 2 with omelette. When assembling the nigiri with omelette, do not add wasabi: instead, tie with a thin nori ribbon, about ½ cm/¼ inch wide.

Arrange on a platter and serve with pickled ginger and Japanese soy sauce in a small dish. Alternatively, serve as party canapés or on small plates as part of a meal.

sushi balls with roast pork & pickled plums

Pickled plums (*umeboshi*) can be bought in Japanese and Asian supermarkets. They can be very salty and sharp, so you don't need too much. If you do not like the flavour of pickled plum, replace with pickled ginger.

250 g/9 oz. pork fillet/ tenderloin, in one piece

2 tablespoons Japanese soy sauce (shoyu)

1 tablespoon mirin (sweetened Japanese rice wine)

1 teaspoon Chinese hot pepper sauce or chilli sauce

½ recipe vinegared rice (see page 13)

10 Japanese pickled plums (umeboshi), halved and pitted

makes 20 pieces

Put the pork in a plastic container. Mix the soy, mirin and hot pepper sauce in a bowl or jug/pitcher, then pour over the pork. Set aside to marinate for 1 hour, turning the pork in the marinade every 15 minutes.

Preheat the oven to 200°C (400°F) Gas 6.

Put the pork in a roasting pan and pour the marinade over the top. Roast in the preheated oven for 15 minutes. Remove from the oven, let cool, then slice thinly – you should get about 20 slices.

Divide the rice into 20 balls. Take a piece of pickled plum and push it into the centre of a rice ball, then mould the rice around it so it is completely hidden. Repeat with the remaining plums and rice. Top each ball with a slice of the marinated roast pork.

marinated beef sushi

Beef *tataki* is very rare marinated beef served on seasoned sushi rice. If you do not like very rare beef, cook the fillet in a preheated oven at 180°C (350°F) Gas 4 for 10 minutes before returning to the pan to coat with sauce.

2 teaspoons peanut oil

300 g/10½ oz. beef eye fillet, in one piece

2 tablespoons Japanese soy sauce (shoyu)

2 tablespoons mirin (sweetened Japanese rice wine)

2 tablespoons rice vinegar

½ recipe vinegared rice (see page 13)

shredded pickled ginger (see page 17), to serve (optional)

pickled red cabbage

175 g/6 oz. (about ⅛) red cabbage

100 g/½ cup brown sugar

125 ml/½ cup red wine vinegar

makes 18 pieces

To make the pickled red cabbage, finely slice the cabbage, removing any large core pieces, and chop into 2.5-cm/1-inch lengths. Put in a medium saucepan, then add the brown sugar, vinegar and 4 tablespoons water. Bring to the boil, reduce the heat and simmer for 30 minutes.

Remove from the heat, let cool and store in a sealed container in the refrigerator for up to 1 week, or in the freezer for 3 months.

To prepare the beef, heat the oil in a frying pan and sear the beef on all sides until browned. Mix the soy sauce, mirin and vinegar in a bowl and pour over the beef, turning the beef to coat. Remove immediately from the heat and transfer the beef and its sauce to a dish. Let cool, cover and refrigerate for 1 hour, turning once.

Divide the rice into 18 balls, the size of a walnut, and shape into firm ovals.

Cut the beef in half lengthways (along the natural separation line), then slice as finely as possible. Wrap a piece of beef around the top of a rice ball and top with a little pickled cabbage or ginger.

pickled courgette roll with beetroot sashimi

A thinly sliced ribbon of courgette/zucchini makes a stunning alternative to nori on the outside of a sushi roll. It is easiest to cut the courgette and beetroot/beet using a mandoline - the plastic Japanese ones are marvellous - but if you don't have one you can use a sharp peeler or knife and a steady hand.

3 medium courgettes/zucchini (green or yellow, or both)

1–2 very small beetroot/beets or 5–6 baby beetroot/beets, uncooked

1 teaspoon wasabi paste

1½ tablespoons Japanese mayonnaise

½ recipe vinegared rice (see page 13)

pickling mixture

250 ml/1 cup Japanese rice vinegar

60 g/⅓ cup sugar

2 tablespoons mirin (sweetened Japanese rice wine)

hand vinegar

4 tablespoons Japanese rice vinegar

250 ml/1 cup water

dipping sauce

2 tablespoons Japanese mild soy sauce

1 tablespoon sake

makes 18 pieces

Mix the hand vinegar ingredients in a small bowl and set aside.

To make the pickling mixture, put the vinegar, sugar and mirin in a small saucepan and bring to the boil, stirring. Reduce to a simmer and cook for 5 minutes. Remove from the heat and let cool.

Thinly slice the courgettes lengthways, discarding the first and last couple of pieces (they will be too narrow). Arrange the slices flat in a shallow dish or container and pour the pickling mixture over the top. Set aside for 4 hours or overnight.

When ready to assemble the sushi, peel the raw beetroot and slice carefully, as thinly as possible.

Put the wasabi and mayonnaise in a small bowl and mix well.

Dip your fingers in the hand vinegar. Divide the seasoned rice into 18 portions about the size of a walnut, and shape each piece into a flattened ball. Wrap a ribbon of pickled courgette around the outside of each piece, top with a dab of wasabi mayonnaise and thin slivers of raw beetroot.

To make the dipping sauce, mix the soy sauce and sake together and serve in a small bowl beside the sushi.

mackerel sushi pieces

Battera, a speciality from Osaka, is one of the most popular sushi in Japan. It is made in a container or moulded into a log with a sushi mat and cut into small pieces. In restaurants and shops it often comes wrapped up with a transparent sheet of kombu (dried kelp).

1 medium fresh mackerel, about 400 g/14 oz., filleted

3–4 tablespoons Japanese rice vinegar

sea salt

½ recipe vinegared rice (see page 13)

pickled ginger (see page 17), to serve

Japanese soy sauce (shoyu), to serve

a wooden mould or rectangular plastic container, 18 x 12 x 5 cm/ 7 x 4½ x 2 inches

makes 16 pieces

Start the preparation for this dish a few hours before cooking the rice. Take a dish larger than the fish fillets and cover with a thick layer of salt. Put the mackerel fillets, flesh side down, on top of the salt and cover completely with more salt. Set aside for 3–4 hours. Remove the mackerel and rub off the salt with damp kitchen paper. Carefully remove all the bones with tweezers, then put into a dish and pour the rice vinegar over the fillets. Leave to marinate for 30 minutes.

Using your fingers, carefully remove the transparent skin from each fillet, starting at the tail end. Put the fillets, skin side down, on a cutting board and slice off the highest part from the centre of the flesh so the fillets will be fairly flat. Keep the trimmings.

Line a wet wooden mould or rectangular container with a large piece of clingfilm/plastic wrap.

Put a fillet, skin side down, in the mould or container. Fill the gaps with the other fillet and trimmings. Press the cooked rice down firmly on top of the fish (dip your fingers in hand vinegar if the rice is sticking to them). Put the wet wooden lid on top, or fold in the clingfilm/plastic wrap and put a piece of cardboard and a weight on top.

You can leave it in a cool place (not the refrigerator) for a few hours. When ready to serve, remove from the container and unwrap any clingfilm/plastic wrap. Take a very sharp knife and wipe it with a vinegar-soaked cloth or piece of kitchen paper. Cut the block of sushi in 4 lengthways, then in 4 crossways, making 16 pieces in all.

Arrange on a plate, and serve with pickled ginger and a little soy sauce in small individual dishes.

smoked fish sushi

Oshi-zushi (pressed sushi) like this, or *Bo-zushi* (log sushi) will keep for up to 36 hours – as a result, they are the best-selling items at all Japanese airports. Travellers buy them for Japanese friends living abroad as a reminder of the true taste of Japan. They are easy to make and can be made the day before.

150 g/5 oz. smoked rainbow trout or smoked salmon, thickly sliced

2 slices lemon, cut into 16 fan-shaped pieces

½ recipe vinegared rice (see page 13)

pickled ginger (see page 17), to serve

Japanese soy sauce (shoyu), to serve

a wooden mould or rectangular plastic container, 18 x 12 x 5 cm/ 7 x 4½ x 2 inches

makes 16 pieces

Lay the trout or salmon slices evenly in the bottom of a wet wooden mould. Alternatively, use a rectangular plastic container lined with a piece of clingfilm/plastic wrap large enough for the edges to hang out of the container.

Transfer the vinegared rice into the mould and press it firmly and evenly into the mould (dip your fingers in hand vinegar if the rice is sticking to them). Put the wet wooden lid on top. If using a plastic container, fold in the clingfilm/plastic wrap to cover the rice and top with a piece of cardboard just big enough to cover the rice, and put a weight on top. Leave in a cool place (not the refrigerator) for 2–3 hours or overnight.

When ready to serve, remove from the container and unwrap any clingfilm/ plastic wrap. Take a very sharp knife and wipe it with a vinegar-soaked cloth or kitchen paper. Cut the block of sushi into 4 lengthways, then in 4 crossways, making 16 pieces.

Arrange on a large serving plate. Put a fan-shaped piece of lemon on top. Serve with pickled ginger and a little Japanese soy sauce.

stars, hearts & flowers

Just like cookies, these children's sushi are made in pretty colours and shapes. Specially shaped moulds are sold in Japanese stores, but if you don't have access to such exciting shops, use decorative cookie cutters and other mould shapes.

½ recipe vinegared rice
(see page 13)

cherry blossom sushi

100 g/4 oz. cod or haddock
fillet, skinned

2 tablespoons sugar

sea salt and pepper

red vegetable food colouring*

spring green sushi

100 g/4 oz. shelled green peas

2 teaspoons sugar

sea salt

golden star sushi

2 eggs, beaten

1 tablespoon milk

1 tablespoon sugar

star, daisy and diamond or heart shaped sushi moulds, or cookie cutters

makes 18–20 pieces

*If you don't want to use food colouring, use grilled fresh salmon, flaked, instead of the white fish and colouring.

Put the fish in a saucepan, add just enough boiling water to cover and simmer until well cooked. Drain, then carefully remove all the small bones. Pat dry with kitchen paper and put into the dry saucepan. Using a fork, crush into fine flakes. Add the sugar and a pinch of salt, then cook over a low heat, continuously stirring with a fork, for about 2 minutes, or until the fish is very dry and flaky. If using food colouring, dilute 1 drop with 1 tablespoon water, then stir quickly through the fish to spread the colour evenly. Remove from the heat and let cool. (Alternatively, use fresh salmon cooked to flakes in the same way or crush canned cooked red salmon into flakes.)

Bring a small saucepan of lightly salted water to the boil, add the peas and cook for 5 minutes or until soft. Drain and pat dry with kitchen paper. Crush with a mortar and pestle or in a food processor to form a smooth green paste. Stir in the sugar and a pinch of salt.

Lightly oil a small saucepan and heat over a moderate heat. Put the eggs, milk and sugar in a bowl, mix, then pour into the pan. Quickly stir with a fork to make soft scrambled eggs. Remove from the heat and let cool.

Divide the vinegared rice into three. To make the cherry blossom sushi, put 1 tablespoon of the pink fish flakes in the bottom of a small heart-shaped mould and press about 1 tablespoon of the rice on top. Turn out onto a plate, fish side up. Repeat until all the pink flakes and a third of the rice are used. Using a second mould, repeat using the green pea paste and another third of the rice. Using a third mould, repeat using the scrambled eggs with the remaining third of the rice. If using grilled fresh salmon, use a fourth mould.

Arrange the cherry blossom, flower, star and spring green sushi on a large plate and serve.

egg cup sushi

Hand-moulding of rice is rather a messy job and it's also difficult to make identical shapes and sizes. This simple solution uses an egg cup as a mould. These sushi are very easy to make, pretty to serve and delicious to eat.

¼ recipe vinegared rice
(see page 13)

5–6 smoked salmon slices, about 125 g/4½ oz., halved to make 10–12 pieces

lemon or lime wedges, to serve

a small egg cup

makes 10–12 pieces

Line an egg cup with clingfilm/plastic wrap so it hangs over the edge of the cup. Line the whole cup with a piece of smoked salmon, filling any gaps with small pieces of salmon. Put 1 tablespoon of vinegared rice in the cup and press down gently with your thumbs. Do not over-fill. Trim the excess salmon from the rim. Lift up the clingfilm/plastic wrap and turn out the moulded sushi, upside down, onto a plate. Repeat to make 10 pieces.

Arrange on a serving platter, add lemon or lime wedges and serve.

Variation Make soft scrambled eggs, using 2 eggs, 1 teaspoon sugar and a pinch of salt. Let cool. Lay a piece of clingfilm/plastic wrap in the egg cup. Put 1 teaspoon of the scrambled eggs on the bottom. Gently press to make a firm base – the egg should come about halfway up the side of the cup. Put 1 tablespoon of vinegared rice on top of the egg and again gently press down with your thumbs. Do not over-fill. Using the clingfilm/plastic wrap, turn out the moulded sushi, upside down, onto a plate. Repeat this process for the remainder of the egg and rice. Serve with a tiny bit of red caviar on top.

chilli squid sushi

Squid is delicious in sushi, but can be tricky when raw, because it does tend to be tough. If you braise it slowly, you end up with deliciously tender pieces.

250 g/8 oz. baby squid tubes, 8 cm/3 inches long (about 12), cleaned

1 teaspoon mirin (sweetened Japanese rice wine)

1 teaspoon Japanese soy sauce (shoyu)

½ teaspoon finely chopped fresh red chilli/chile

½ teaspoon finely chopped garlic

1 teaspoon grated fresh ginger

1 tablespoon finely chopped fresh coriander/cilantro

½ recipe vinegared rice (see page 13)

1 tablespoon black sesame seeds

hand vinegar

4 tablespoons Japanese rice vinegar

250 ml/1 cup water

a baking sheet with sides or grill/broiler pan

makes 24 pieces

Slice the squid tubes in half lengthways and arrange on an oven tray or grill tray. Sprinkle with the mirin and soy. Set the tray at least 15 cm/ 6 inches away from a preheated grill/broiler so the heat is not too fierce. Grill/broil for about 8 minutes or until the squid turns opaque. Remove and let cool.

Put the squid in a bowl, add the chilli, garlic, ginger and coriander, stir gently, cover and marinate in the refrigerator for 1 hour.

Mix the hand vinegar ingredients in a small bowl and set aside.

Dip your fingers in the hand vinegar and divide the rice into 24 walnut-sized balls.

Top each rice ball with a piece of squid using the natural curl of the squid body to hold it securely. Sprinkle with a few black sesame seeds, then serve.

spam musubi

Spam is very popular in Japan and Korea and is here cooked and caramelized to make the perfect topping for this hand-moulded sushi. When caramelized in a teriyaki-style sauce, Spam has a sweet, salty, smoky flavour which is balanced perfectly by the seasoned sticky white rice.

200-g/7-oz. can Spam

3 tablespoons Japanese soy sauce (shoyu)

2 tablespoons mirin (sweetened Japanese rice wine)

2 tablespoons sugar

¾ recipe vinegared rice (see page 13)

1 tablespoon furikake seasoning

2 sheets of nori seaweed, each sheet cut into 3 strips 5 cm/2 inches wide

vegetable oil, for frying

makes 6 large pieces

Slice the Spam into six slices, approx 5 mm/¼ inch thick.

Heat some oil in a non-stick frying pan/skillet and fry the Spam slices for 1–1½ minutes on each side until nicely browned and a bit crispy. Transfer the Spam slices to a plate and drain the pan.

Reduce the heat and add the soy sauce, mirin and sugar to the pan. Mix well. Return the Spam slices to the pan and coat well in the sauce, simmering for 1–1½ minutes so the sauce thickens and caramelizes. Remove from the heat.

To create the musubi, shape the cooked rice into six little pillows, approx. 8 x 5 cm/3¼ x 2 inches and roughly 4 cm/1½ inches high. Sprinkle a little furikake on top of each rice pillow and top with a slice of Spam.

Place a strip of nori seaweed, shiny side down, on a clean, dry surface. Lay a musubi across the centre of the nori and fold the nori strip around the width of the musubi so it wraps around the Spam and rice, holding them both together. Using a little water on the tip of your finger, dampen the end of the nori strip and stick it down. Repeat with the rest.

Serve immediately or wrap in clingfilm/plastic wrap and take out with you as a snack.

Tip If you wish, place a fried egg or scrambled egg omelette on top of the Spam before wrapping in the nori.

smoked salmon temaki

A perfect sushi for parties. Serve the rice, nori sheets and prepared ingredients on plates and let people roll their own. Choose ingredients with varied tastes and colours. This is a delicious variation of the hand roll using smoked salmon instead of crabsticks.

4 sheets of nori seaweed or 8 salad leaves

¾ recipe vinegared rice (see page 13)

pickled ginger (see page 17), to serve

hand roll fillings

125 g/4 oz. smoked salmon

4 spring onions/scallions

6 cm/2½ inches pickled daikon (*takuan*)

1 avocado

freshly squeezed juice of 1 lemon

makes 8 rolls

Cut the smoked salmon lengthways into 5 mm/⅛-inch wide strips.

Finely slice the spring onions lengthways into 8–10-cm/3–4-inch strips. Slice the pickled daikon thinly.

Cut the avocado in half, remove the stone and peel carefully. Thinly slice the flesh and brush with lemon juice.

Toast the nori sheets by quickly passing over a low flame or a hotplate to make them crisp and bring out the flavour. Cut each sheet in half crossways.

Put the rice in a serving bowl and arrange the salmon, spring onion and avocado on a platter. Serve them with the nori and pickled ginger on small separate plates.

To assemble, follow the step-by-step directions on the following pages.

assembling hand rolls step by step

1 Take one piece of nori seaweed in one hand and add 2-3 tablespoons of vinegared rice. Spread the rice over half the nori.

2 Arrange your choice of fillings diagonally over the rice from the centre to the outer corner.

1

2

3

4

3 Take the bottom right-hand corner and curl it towards the middle to form a cone.

4 Keep rolling the cone until complete. To glue the cone closed (optional), put a few grains of rice on the edge of the nori, and press together.

5 When the cone is complete, add your choice of a few drops of soy sauce, a few pieces of pickled ginger and a dab of wasabi paste.

5

mini crab & cucumber rolls

Oboro are fine white fish flakes, usually coloured pink, making them perfect for adding a splash of colour to sushi. These tiny hand rolls are very easy to eat with your fingers, and so make perfect party food. If you mix all the ingredients before rolling the sushi, the process will be a lot easier.

7 cm/3 inch piece of cucumber

150 g/6 oz. crabmeat

1 small or ½ medium (firm) avocado, cut into small cubes

½ recipe vinegared rice (see page 13)

6–7 sheets of nori seaweed

1 teaspoon wasabi paste (optional)

1 tablespoon *oboro* (optional, see recipe introduction)

makes 60–70 rolls

Slice the cucumber in half lengthways and scrape out the seeds. Chop the flesh into tiny cubes and put in a bowl. Add the crabmeat, avocado and rice and mix gently.

Cut each sheet of nori in half lengthways, then cut the halves into 5 pieces crossways (9 x 4 cm/4 x 1½ inches).

Put 1 piece of nori, rough side up with the long edge towards you, on a work surface. Spread 1 teaspoon of the rice mixture crossways over the nori about quarter of the way in from the left edge. Smear the rice with a little wasabi, if using. Take the bottom left corner of the nori and fold it diagonally so the left edge meets the top edge, then continue folding the whole triangle. Sprinkle the open end with a little oboro, if using. Repeat until all the ingredients have been used.

smoked fish hand roll

This larger hand roll is still small enough to be held and eaten easily, but also makes a great starter or lunch if you allow three rolls per person. Choose any smoked fish, but make sure it is moist and soft.

1 small red onion, finely sliced

1 tablespoon rice vinegar

180 g/7 oz. smoked fish, such as trout, salmon or eel

5-cm/2-inch piece of cucumber

6 sheets of nori seaweed, about 21 x 18 cm/8 x 7 inches

½ recipe vinegared rice (see page 13)

1 teaspoon wasabi paste (optional)

1 small carrot, finely sliced into thin strips

1 small red (bell) pepper, finely sliced into thin strips

Japanese soy sauce (shoyu), to serve

makes 18 rolls

Put the onion in a small saucepan with the vinegar and 4 tablespoons water. Bring to the boil, drain and let cool.

Cut the smoked fish into even strips, about 6 x 1 cm/2 x ½ inch long – you should have 18 even pieces.

Quarter the cucumber lengthways, scrape out the seeds, then cut into fine strips.

Cut each sheet of nori into 3 pieces (18 x 7 cm/7 x 3 inches).

Put a piece of nori, rough side up with the long edge towards you. Spread 1 small heaped teaspoon of rice crossways over the nori about a quarter of the way in from the left edge. Smear with a little wasabi, if using. Top the rice with a piece of fish, a few strips of carrot, red pepper and cucumber and a little red onion, pressing slightly into the rice to hold it firm while you roll.

Take the bottom left corner of the nori and fold it diagonally so the left edge meets the top edge. Continue folding the whole triangle. Arrange with the join downwards on a serving plate or tray. Repeat to make 18 rolls altogether. Serve with soy sauce.

mushroom sushi cones

Sushi cones are a stylish way to use tiny Japanese mushrooms like hon-shigiri and enoki. Their delicate clusters of nodding heads would be completely lost in a rolled sushi.

4 sheets of nori seaweed, halved (10 x 17 cm/ 4 x 7 inches) and toasted over a gas flame or hotplate

½ recipe vinegared rice (see page 13)

Japanese soy sauce (shoyu), to serve

fillings such as

enoki mushrooms, raw or smoked salmon, blanched asparagus, finely sliced carrot, cucumber strips, thin Japanese omelette (page 14), sliced, sesame seeds, wasabi and pickled ginger (see page 17)

makes about 20 cones

Put a sheet of nori, shiny side down, on a work surface. Put 1 tablespoon rice on the left edge. Using wet hands, spread it lightly to cover half the seaweed completely.

Add your choice of filling ingredaients diagonally across the rice, letting them overlap the top left corner.

To roll the cones, put one finger in the middle of the bottom edge, then roll up the cone from the bottom left, using your finger as the axis of the turn. As each cone is made, wet the outer edge with a finger dipped in vinegar, add a dot of rice to help seal it, then roll shut. Put on a serving platter with the join side down.

Serve with soy sauce for dipping.

avocado & prawn wraps

These wraps are best made as close to eating as possible, ideally within an hour as the nori will soften once filled. For hands-on entertaining, provide separate dishes of the individual ingredients, plus the cooked rice and nori sheets, and let everyone make their own wraps, choosing their favourite fillings.

½ small avocado

1 tablespoon freshly squeezed lemon juice

½ recipe vinegared rice (see page 13)

4 sheets of nori seaweed, each cut into four

2 tablespoons wasabi paste

100 g/4 oz. fresh tuna fillet, cut into 8 fingers

½ yellow bell pepper, deseeded and cut into sticks

50 g/2 oz. smoked salmon slices, cut into 8 pieces

8 cooked and shelled tiger prawns/shrimp

6-cm/2½-inch piece cucumber, cut into sticks

pickled ginger (see page 17), to serve

Japanese soy sauce (shoyu), to serve

makes 16 wraps

Peel the avocado and cut it into slices. Put the lemon juice in a shallow dish, add the avocado and toss to coat.

Spread 2 tablespoons of rice over a piece of nori. Add a small amount of wasabi paste and top with a piece each of tuna, pepper and avocado. You may find this easier if you hold the nori on the palm of your hand to fill. Roll up into a cone shape. Dampen the final edge with water or shoyu sauce to stick together. Fill 7 more squares of nori in the same way.

Fill the remaining nori squares with rice topped with a smoked salmon piece, a prawn/shrimp and a couple of cucumber sticks. Serve the sushi wraps with small dishes of pickled ginger and shoyu sauce.

temaki rolls with fermented seed pâté

This hand-rolled sushi is really easy to make. Temakis are a great choice for sushi parties since they are best rolled directly at the table, just before eating, and everybody can join in, which leaves you with less work! Prepare and serve all ingredients in the middle of the table and let the fun begin!

for the pâté
(makes 250 g/2½ cups)

240 g/2 cups pumpkin seeds

50 ml/scant ¼ cup olive oil

1 garlic clove

¼ teaspoon ground turmeric

1 tablespoon nutritional yeast (optional)

3 teaspoons rice or barley miso

2 teaspoons lemon juice

¼ teaspoon salt

freshly crushed black pepper

for the rolls

6 sheets of nori seaweed, halved

2 carrots, julienned

300 g/2 cups sauerkraut or other fermented vegetables

1 ripe avocado, halved, pitted/ stoned and cut into strips

3 spring onions/scallions, cut into 10-cm/4-inch pieces

2 handfuls rocket/arugula or 50 g/1 cup alfalfa sprouts

makes 12 rolls

First make the pâté. Soak the pumpkin seeds in 840 ml/3½ cups water (preferably non-chlorinated) for 2–3 days, until slightly fermented, without changing the soaking water. Discard the soaking water and rinse them thoroughly under running water. Drain well.

Place the soaked seeds in a high-speed blender jug/pitcher, together with the remaining ingredients and 60 ml/¼ cup water. Blend until smooth, using a tamper tool to push down the ingredients. If you don't own a high-speed blender, the pâté will probably turn out chunkier in a less powerful blender, and more water will need to be added, resulting in a somewhat runnier consistency. Do not halve this recipe, since the blender needs the amount of at least 2 cups in order to make a smooth paste. Let sit in the fridge for another day; the flavours really develop in this final stage of setting. There will be some leftovers, but you can easily store this pâté in the fridge and use it as a dip or as a spread within a week.

Make sure your hands are dry before starting. Place a piece of nori (shiny side down) in the palm of your hand and add 1½ tablespoons of pumpkin seed pâté. Spread it gently on the left third of the nori sheet. Place your chosen fillings diagonally over the pate. Do not overfill; a couple of carrot matchsticks, 1 slice of avocado, 1 tablespoon of sauerkraut and some greens are more than enough. Fold the bottom left corner of the nori over and begin rolling into a cone shape. Wet the edge with little water and seal. Continue until all the nori is used.

Serve the temaki rolls with more fermented vegetables, condiments, some soy sauce and leftover greens.

quinoa wraps

Sushi is well known as a healthy choice, but the traditional white sushi rice is usually prepared with white sugar. If you prefer a sugar-free version, using quinoa is a good option. Plus this is a great way to use up quinoa or any other leftover grains from last night's dinner.

80 g/¾ cup cooked quinoa

2 teaspoons rice vinegar

4 sheets of nori seaweed, about 20 x 20 cm/8 x 8 inches

2 carrots

10-cm/4-inch piece of cucumber

½ avocado

2–3 spring onions/scallions

handful of beansprouts

handful of microgreens, such as mizuna, pea shoots, or watercress (optional)

1 teaspoon black or white sesame seeds

3 tablespoons tamari soy sauce

wasabi, to serve (optional)

pickled ginger (see page 17), to serve (optional)

makes 8 wraps

Put the quinoa and rice vinegar in a bowl and toss to coat.

Cut the nori sheets in half diagonally so that you have 8 triangular pieces. Cut the carrots and cucumber into matchsticks. Cut the avocado in half and make fine slices into the flesh, then peel off the skin. Chop the spring onions.

Take one nori triangle and spoon 1 tablespoon of the quinoa in a line along one of the short sides of the triangle. Place a few carrot and cucumber matchsticks on top, 2 or 3 slices of the avocado, a few beansprouts and microgreens, if using, and some spring onions. Try to put a greater portion of the vegetables towards what will be the larger end of your sushi cone. Roll the nori up all around the filling, then scatter a few sesame seeds at the mouth of the cone. Repeat with the rest of the nori pieces.

Serve with soy sauce, wasabi and pickled ginger, if using.

6 sashimi

mixed sashimi with ginger soy dressing & micro herbs

Salmon and tuna are used for this pretty sashimi with ginger soy dressing and micro herb garnish. Ask your fishmonger for the very best, freshest fish he has to offer. If you prefer, you can sear the fish quickly in a smoking-hot frying pan.

250 g/8 oz. sushi-grade tuna fillet

250 g/8 oz. skinless salmon fillet, pin bones removed

5-cm/2-inch piece of mooli/daikon radish

4 red-skinned radishes, trimmed

4 spring onions/scallions, trimmed

1 tablespoon pickled ginger

micro herbs, baby rocket/arugula, or fresh coriander/cilantro

ginger soy dressing

½ fresh red chilli/chile, finely chopped

½–1 teaspoon wasabi paste

2 tablespoons Japanese soy sauce (shoyu)

freshly squeezed juice of ½ lime

serves 4

Cut the fish into thin slices and arrange on a platter.

Peel and cut the mooli into fine matchsticks. Cut the radishes into fine matchsticks. Thinly slice the spring onions. Mix the mooli, radishes and spring onionss together and add to the platter. Add the pickled ginger, too.

To make the ginger soy dressing, mix together the chopped chilli, wasabi paste, soy sauce and lime juice in a little bowl.

Garnish the sashimi with the micro herbs and serve immediately with the ginger soy dressing.

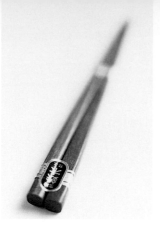

seared tuna sashimi salad

You may take some time to get used to the idea of eating completely raw fish, but lightly blanched or seared fillet with salad is a good starting point. You can use other fish such as turbot, salmon or swordfish.

200 g/8 oz. fresh tuna or swordfish, skinned

iced water

green salad leaves

a small clump of enoki mushrooms, trimmed and separated

wasabi dressing

freshly squeezed juice of 1 lemon

2 teaspoons wasabi paste

1½ tablespoons Japanese soy sauce (shoyu)

serves 4

Grill the tuna or swordfish at a high heat for about 1 minute on each side until the surfaces are seared but the inside is still raw. Plunge into iced water. Drain and pat dry with paper towels. Slice into 5-mm/⅛-inch thick pieces.

Mix the lemon juice, wasabi and soy sauce in a small bowl and set aside.

Arrange the salad leaves and enoki mushrooms in the centre of a large serving plate and arrange the seared fish over the leaves. Just before serving, pour the wasabi dressing over the top.

sesame seared tuna with asian slaw

40 g/⅓ cup mixed black and white sesame seeds

2 x 170-g/6-oz sushi grade tuna pieces

2 tablespoons grapeseed oil

sea salt and freshly ground black pepper

for the asian slaw

250 g/1 cup jícama, sliced in long strips (or use carrots if you cannot get hold of jicama)

½ mango, sliced in long strips

100 g/2 packed cups thinly sliced red cabbage

tamari sauce

1 tablespoon Japanese soy sauce (shoyu)

2 teaspoons sesame oil

¼ teaspoon finely sliced ginger

2 teaspoons flaxseed oil

2 teaspoons clear honey

1 tablespoon freshly squeezed lemon juice

1 tablespoon white sesame seeds

a handful of fresh coriander/ cilantro, to garnish

serves 4

Walk into your local sushi chain and it's easy to see that sesame seeds are often used for presentation. But they actually give a nutritional punch of calcium and magnesium as well, so are definitely worthwhile using.

Spread the black and white sesame seeds evenly on a plate. Season each side of tuna with salt and pepper. Then coat each side of the tuna with the seed mixture – don't forget the sides as well. In a grill pan, heat the grapeseed oil over medium-high heat. Once the oil is hot, sear the tuna for 30 seconds on all 4 sides. Remove from the pan and set aside.

For the asian slaw, cut the jícama, mango and cabbage into long strips.

Whisk all the ingredients for the tamari sauce together in a bowl. Add the slaw and mix it all together.

To serve, thinly slice the tuna steak. Spoon a generous amount of slaw on each plate and place the sliced tuna on top. Garnish with fresh coriander.

sashimi & cucumber bites

600 g/1 lb. 5 oz. fresh or sashimi-grade fish (tuna is classic, but to avoid eating over-fished tuna, you can substitute any other sashimi-grade fish)

½ teaspoon sugar

3 tablespoons Japanese soy sauce (shoyu)

1 tablespoon sesame oil

1 tablespoon grated fresh ginger

1 tablespoon finely chopped red chilli/chile

35 g/½ cup (about 5) chopped spring onions/scallions

1 tablespoon black sesame seeds

1 tablespoon white sesame seeds

1 large avocado, diced into 1-cm/½-inch dice

1 cucumber, slightly hollowed out, cut into thick slices, to serve

serves 6–8

A little bit of chilli keeps things sprightly in this fresh and tasty sashimi mix that is used to top thick slices of cucumber to make a crunchy and delicious snack. You could also serve the sashimi mix in lettuce cups as an alternative.

Trim any sinew or bloodlines off the pieces of fish. Cut the flesh into 1-cm/¾-inch dice.

Stir the sugar into the soy sauce until it dissolves. Mix with the sesame oil, ginger and chilli. Combine the soy dressing with the fish. Gently fold through the spring onions, sesame seeds and avocado.

Mix the diced fish into the dressing and then pile onto thick slices of cucumber to serve.

Tip To make this heartier, serve with warm sticky white rice made just before serving.

poke inari cups

The essential thing here is a Japanese slant on the poke itself, served in their wraps, and garnished with Japanese favourites. Ideal for parties as a canapé, especially if you use a variety of poke fillings to make an eye-catching platter of bites.

12 inari sushi pockets (also called inari pouches or wraps)

1 recipe vinegared rice (see page 13)

200 g/7 oz. prawn/shrimp poke (see below)

for the prawn/shrimp poke

500 g/1 lb. 2 oz. very fresh raw prawns/shrimp, peeled

freshly squeezed juice of 1 lime

2 teaspoons yuzu

2 tablespoons coriander seeds

1 red onion, very thinly sliced

2 tablespoons Japanese soy sauce (shoyu)

1 teaspoon chia seeds

1 teaspoon crumbed nori seaweed

to serve

2 tablespoons fish roe (*tobiko*)

2 tablespoons nori seaweed

3 tablespoons bean curd

3 spring onions/scallions, finely sliced

sriracha

3 small chillies/chiles, finely diced

serves 4

To make the prawn/shrimp poke, place the raw peeled prawns/shrimp in a bowl with the lime juice and yuzu. Marinate for 30–60 minutes.

Toast the coriander seeds in a dry frying pan/skillet, stirring to ensure they do not burn, then grind using a pestle and mortar. Add to the marinade with the red onion for the final 15 minutes of marinating. When ready to serve, add the shoyu, chia seeds and nori seaweed.

Take an inari pouch and shape into a top-loadable cup. Put a little sushi rice in the bottom, fill with a choice of up to three different fish pokes. Add tobiko, nori and a small amount of bean curd, and top with spring onions/scallions. Repeat to make 11 more cups. Pour a little poke marinade into each cup to moisten.

Typically serve individually as canapés or as a plate of three different pockets. Have sriracha, finely diced chillies/chiles and more marinade on the side for seasoning to taste.

Note Make different poke variations, by replacing the prawns/shrimp with ahi, tuna and/or smoked albacore and use them to create a variety of filled inari pouches.

seared fish bites

This is a variation on a sashimi type of sushi with an added layer of nori seaweed to give that extra umami element. The recipe can just as easily be made without the nori though and with pork, chicken, squid or another fish (such as mahi mahi/ dorado or even cod or halibut) instead of the 'ahi.

900 g/2 lb. 'ahi or yellowfin tuna fillets

1 tablespoon salt

1 tablespoon freshly ground black pepper

130 g/1 cup plain/all-purpose flour

4 eggs

100 g/2 cups panko breadcrumbs

8 sheets of nori seaweed

vegetable oil, for frying

for the sauce

100 ml/⅓ cup light Japanese soy sauce (shoyu)

2 tablespoons dry mustard, mixed with a little water to make a paste

225 g/1 cup mayonnaise

to serve

steamed white rice

furikake seasoning

serves 12

Cut the fish into slices roughly 18 cm/7 inches long and 2.5 cm/1 inch thick.

You will need three wide, shallow bowls. In the first bowl, mix the salt, pepper and flour. Break the eggs into the second bowl and beat them with a fork. Put all the panko breadcrumbs into the third bowl.

Wrap each fillet of fish in a sheet of nori so the seaweed overlaps. Lightly wet the tip of your finger in water and run it along the edge of the nori to help it stick and stay wrapped around the 'ahi. Dip each fillet into the flour mixture, then in the egg wash and finally coat with the panko breadcrumbs.

Shallow-fry the breadcrumbed fillets in vegetable oil over a medium heat, for 2–3 minutes on each side, turning frequently until evenly browned and golden. Place on a plate covered in paper towels to drain away the excess oil, then slice.

For the sauce, mix together the shoyu, mustard paste and mayonnaise and serve as a side sauce, along with some steamed white rice and furikake.

raw fish & chips

This is a take on the favourite British dish, fish and chips. The star of the show is the fresh tuna sashimi in a citrus and ginger dressing that combines beautifully with the salty, crispy chips/fries.

fish

2 teaspoons Japanese soy sauce (shoyu)

1-cm/½-inch piece of ginger, finely chopped

4 tablespoons orange juice

1 teaspoon wasabi paste

1 spring onion/scallion, thinly sliced

200 g/7-oz. line-caught, sashimi-grade tuna

chips/fries

1–2 litres/4–8 cups vegetable oil

400 g/14 oz. Maris Piper/russet potatoes, cut into fat matchsticks

sea salt

wasabi mayo

7 tablespoons mayonnaise

1 teaspoon wasabi paste

deep fat fryer (optional)

serves 2

First, make the fish. Combine the soy sauce, ginger, orange juice and wasabi in a bowl. With a sharp knife, cut the tuna against the grain into tidy 2-cm/1-inch cubes. Marinate in the bowl for 15 minutes.

To make the chips/fries, heat up your deep fat fryer, or a large, deep pan half-filled with oil over medium heat. Heat the oil to 140°C/285°F or until a cube of bread dropped in sizzles and browns in 1 minute.

Deep fry the chips for 3 minutes. Remove from the oil with a slotted spoon and set on a board. Stab them several times with a fork to create crispy bits. Return them to the oil and fry again for 2 minutes or until golden. Remove and drain on a kitchen paper/paper towel. Season with salt.

Make the wasabi mayo, by combining the mayonnaise and wasabi paste.

Scatter the spring onions over the marinated tuna and serve with the chips and wasabi mayo.

7

other small

bites

lettuce boats

As an alternative to hand-moulded sushi, serve nigiri in lettuce 'boats'. They look very pretty and are also easier to pick up and eat – important if serving at a party.

½ recipe vinegared rice (see page 13)

toppings

100 g/4 oz. beef fillet, about 7 cm/3 inches thick

vegetable oil, for rubbing

1–2 rollmops (marinated Bismarck herring)

8 asparagus tips

2 teaspoons wasabi paste or powder

4 Little Gem/romaine lettuce leaves

8 small chicory (witloof)/ Belgian endive leaves

to serve

sprigs of cress or shredded spring onions/scallions

4 small strips of nori seaweed

2.5-cm/1-inch piece fresh ginger, peeled and grated

1 spring onion/scallion, finely chopped

2 tablespoons white wine

1½ tablespoons Japanese soy sauce (shoyu)

freshly squeezed juice of ½ lemon

makes 12 pieces

Rub the beef all over with oil. Grill/broil at a high heat until golden-brown on all sides, but rare in the middle. Plunge into iced water to stop the cooking. Remove from the water, pat dry with kitchen paper and cut 4 thin slices, about 7 x 4 cm/3 x 2 inches. All the slices should be red on the inside and brown around the edges.

Cut the rollmops into 4 and make a little lengthways slit (about 3 cm/ 1¼ inches) in the skin of each piece.

Cook the asparagus in lightly salted water for 5 minutes until soft. Drain and place under running water to arrest cooking and bring out the colour. Pat dry with kitchen paper.

If using wasabi powder, mix with 2 teaspoons water in an egg cup, stir to make a clay-like consistency, then turn upside down to stop it drying out.

Take a handful of the cooked rice in one hand (about 1–2 tablespoons). Mould it into a rectangular shape about 5 x 2.5 x 2.5 cm/2 x 1 x 1 inches. (Dip your fingers in hand vinegar if the rice is sticking to them.) Repeat with the remaining rice, making 12 portions. Put a tiny dab of wasabi on top of 4 of the portions.

Arrange a slice of beef on 1 portion of wasabi-and-rice, with the two short sides hanging over the end. Top with a few sprigs of cress. Repeat with the other 3 slices of beef and set them in 4 lettuce leaves.

Arrange 2 asparagus tips on another rice portion, set it in a chicory and tie with a nori ribbon. Repeat to make 3 more. Arrange a piece of rollmop on each of the remaining 4 rice portions and insert grated ginger and chopped spring onion into the slits.

Arrange all the leaf boats on a serving platter. Mix the white wine, soy sauce and the lemon juice in a small bowl. Serve the lettuce boats with a small bowl of lemon sauce and another of plain soy sauce.

lettuce rolls

Battleship rolls can be made with lettuce leaves instead of nori. Use iceberg to make cups and a lettuce with flexible leaves, such as butter lettuce or lollo rosso, to make ribbons.

4 small lollo rosso or oakleaf lettuce leaves

4 butter lettuce leaves

4 small iceberg lettuce leaves

½ recipe vinegared rice (see page 13)

Japanese soy sauce (shoyu), to serve

hand vinegar

4 tablespoons Japanese rice vinegar

250 ml/1 cup water

toppings

75 g/3 oz. smoked haddock

1 bay leaf

1 teaspoon sugar

75 g/3 oz. smoked salmon, finely chopped

1 tablespoon freshly squeezed lemon juice

4–6 tablespoons black lumpfish caviar

1 tablespoon caperberries or capers, drained

makes 12 pieces

Mix the hand vinegar ingredients in a small bowl and set aside.

Put the haddock and bay leaf in a saucepan, cover with boiling water, return to the boil, then simmer for 5 minutes or until cooked. Drain well. Remove and discard the skin and all the small bones. Put in a bowl and flake finely with a fork. Stir in the sugar and let cool.

Sprinkle the smoked salmon with lemon juice.

Cut 3 cm/1-inch strips crossways from the outside edges of the lollo rosso and butter lettuce leaves. Make small cups, 7 cm/3 inches in diameter, from the inner iceberg leaves.

Make 12 rectangular mounds of rice, following the method on page 49. Instead of wrapping in nori, wrap 4 in lollo rosso leaves, 4 in butter lettuce and 4 in iceberg lettuce cups. Put about 1 tablespoon of haddock flakes on top of the rice in the lollo rosso leaves. Put about 1 tablespoon smoked salmon on the rice in the butter lettuce and about 1 tablespoon caviar in the iceberg cups. Top the haddock with a little caviar, the salmon with a caperberry or caper and the caviar with a few flakes of haddock.

Arrange on a platter or small plates and serve with a dish of soy sauce.

lunchbox sushi mixture

Gomoku-zushi means 'five-kinds sushi' and usually has around 5–8 ingredients. This standard mixture is a popular dish for lunch because it's easy to cook and adjust the amounts.

1 recipe vinegared vice
(see page 13)

toppings

3–4 dried shiitake mushrooms

6 tablespoons/⅓ cup sugar

3 tablespoons Japanese
soy sauce (shoyu)

½ carrot, finely sliced into
2-cm/1-inch strips

200 ml/1 cup chicken stock
or water

1 tablespoon sake

50 g/2 oz. green beans,
trimmed

½ small lotus root (renkon),
(optional)

200 ml/¾ cup Japanese
rice vinegar

2 eggs, beaten

sea salt

sunflower oil, for frying

serves 4–6

Soak the shiitakes in warm water for 30 minutes. Drain, retaining the soaking liquid. Remove and discard the stems, then thinly slice the caps. Put in a small saucepan, cover with 100 ml/1 scant cup soaking liquid, 2 tablespoons sugar and 2 tablespoons soy sauce. Simmer for 10 minutes or until most of the liquid disappears. Transfer to a bowl and let cool.

Put the carrot in a saucepan with water to cover. Bring to the boil, then drain in a colander. Put the chicken stock or water in the pan, add the remaining soy sauce and sake, bring to the boil, add the carrot and cook for 3–4 minutes. Transfer to a bowl and let cool.

Add some salted water to the saucepan, bring to the boil, add the beans and boil for 2 minutes until just soft. Drain and cool under running water. Pat dry with paper towels and slice diagonally into 5-cm/2-inch long shreds.

Peel the lotus root, if using, and slice into thin rings. Bring a small saucepan of water to the boil, add 1 tablespoon rice vinegar and the lotus root and boil until just soft. Drain and transfer to a mixing bowl. Put the remaining rice vinegar in the saucepan, add the remaining sugar and 2 teaspoons salt, bring to the boil and stir until dissolved. Remove from the heat, add to the lotus root and let marinate for 15–20 minutes.

Beat the eggs with a pinch of salt. Heat a frying pan/skillet, brush with sunflower oil, add the egg and cook until just set. Transfer the egg pancake to a cutting board and cut into fine shreds, 5-cm/2-inches long.

Put the rice in a bowl and fold in all the ingredients except the egg shreds and a few of the beans. Transfer to bowls or lunchboxes, top with the egg shreds and beans and serve.

omelette parcel sushi

A *fukusa* is an elaborate napkin used for the traditional Japanese tea ceremony. It is folded in various ways and is an important part of the classic performance. It has lent its name to this folded pancake sushi as it is commonly known as *fukusa-zushi*.

10 eggs, beaten

2 tablespoons sugar

½ teaspoon sea salt

1 teaspoon cornflour/
cornstarch blended with
1 teaspoon water

2 tablespoons sesame seeds
(black or white)

½ recipe vinegared rice
(see page 13)

50 g/2 oz. anchovy fillets,
finely chopped

1 bunch of mizuna (optional)

sunflower oil, for frying

hand vinegar

4 tablespoons/¼ cup Japanese
rice vinegar

250 ml/1 cup water

to serve

pickled ginger (see page 17)

Japanese soy sauce (shoyu)

*20-cm/8-inch non-stick
frying pan/skillet*

makes 8 parcels

Mix the hand vinegar ingredients in a small bowl and set aside.

Put the eggs in a large mixing bowl and lightly beat with a fork. Strain through a sieve into another bowl. Add the sugar, salt and blended cornflour and mix well until dissolved. Do not whip.

Heat the frying pan/skillet, add a little oil and spread over the base with paper towels. Add 1 small ladle of the egg mixture and spread evenly by tilting the pan. Cook over low heat for 30 seconds on each side until it becomes firm but not browned. Transfer to a plate and let cool. Repeat to make 8 egg pancakes.

Put the sesame seeds in a small saucepan and toss over moderate heat until they start to pop. Remove from the heat and crush coarsely with a mortar and pestle.

While the rice is still warm, fold in the chopped anchovies and crushed sesame seeds. Dip your hands in the hand vinegar, then divide the rice mixture into 8 balls.

Put an egg pancake on a board and put a rice ball in the centre. Fold the front of the pancake over the rice, then fold over the two sides, then the far side, like an envelope. Tuck the edges into the sides. Repeat to make 8 parcels. Alternatively, fold into a money bag, as shown (inset).

If using mizuna to tie the parcels, soak the stems in boiling water for about 30 seconds, and use 2 pieces to tie each parcel. Serve with pickled ginger and soy sauce.

tofu bags

Inari-zushi are small bags made of tofu that make perfect pockets for tasty fillings. *Inari* is actually a shrine dedicated to agriculture and the fox is regarded as the envoy of the god. People used to offer fried beancurd (*abura-age*) to the fox; hence this special name.

½ recipe vinegared rice (see page 13)

3 fresh Japanese fried beancurd (abura-age)

200 ml/¾ cup chicken stock

3 tablespoons sugar

2 tablespoons mirin (sweetened Japanese rice wine) or sweet sherry

2 tablespoons Japanese soy sauce (shoyu)

2 dried shiitake mushrooms

5 cm/2 inches carrot, finely chopped

1 tablespoon sake (optional)

hand vinegar

4 tablespoons/¼ cup Japanese rice vinegar

250 ml/1 cup water

to serve

pickled ginger (see page 17)

Japanese soy sauce (shoyu)

makes 6 tofu bags

Mix the hand vinegar ingredients in a small bowl and set aside.

Put the fried beancurd on a cutting board and roll each one with a rolling pin. This separates the thin layers inside the beancurd, making a bag. Put the beancurd in a mixing bowl, pour over boiling water, then drain – this will reduce the oiliness.

Cut each piece in half and carefully open each piece from the cut side (if not opened already), to make a bag.

Put the chicken stock or water in a saucepan, add 2 tablespoons of the sugar and bring to the boil. Add the beancurd bags, cook for 3 minutes on moderate heat, then add 1 tablespoon mirin and 1 tablespoon soy sauce. Simmer over a low heat for 10 minutes or until all the liquid disappears. Remove from the heat and transfer to a plate.

Meanwhile, soak the dried shiitakes in a bowl of warm water for at least 30 minutes, then drain, reserving the liquid. Cut off the stems and finely chop the caps. Pour 50 ml/¼ cup of the soaking liquid into a saucepan, add the remaining sugar, mirin and soy sauce, and the sake, if using, and bring to the boil. Add the carrot and shiitakes and simmer for 3–4 minutes until almost all the liquid is absorbed. Remove from the heat and let cool.

While the rice is still warm, fold in the cooked carrot and shiitakes. Dip your hands in the hand vinegar and divide the rice mixture into 6 balls. Squeeze out excess juice from the beancurd bags and open with your fingers. Stuff a ball of rice into each bag and fold in the edge (optional). You may cut some bags in half and stuff rice in the corner to make a 3-cornered 'Napoleon's hat' shape. Arrange the bags on a serving plate and serve with pickled ginger and soy sauce.

sushi in a bowl

A bowl of sushi with sashimi on top is a favourite in Tokyo. You can use just one ingredient like tuna, or the assorted sashimi normally used in restaurants, including tuna, prawn/shrimp, eel, sea bass, shellfish, herring roe, salmon roe – almost any good material from the market on the day.

½ recipe vinegared rice
(see page 13)

sashimi: your choice of

2 uncooked tiger prawns/
medium shrimp, peeled but
with tail fins intact

1 octopus tentacle

125 g/4 oz. fresh tuna and/or
salmon

1 turbot, grouper or bass fillet,
about 75 g/3 oz.

1 small squid, cleaned and
skinned

2 large dried shiitake
mushrooms

1 teaspoon sugar

1 teaspoon mirin (sweetened
Japanese rice wine)

sea salt

hand vinegar

4 tablespoons Japanese
rice vinegar

250 ml/1 cup water

to serve

4 cm/2 inches cucumber

pickled ginger (see page 17)

wasabi paste

Japanese soy sauce (shoyu)

serves 2

Bring a saucepan of lightly salted water to the boil, add the prawns and poach for 1–2 minutes until just pink. Remove with a slotted spoon, cool under running water, then pat dry with paper towels.

Return the water to the boil, add the octopus and cook for 7–8 minutes. Drain and cool under running water. Pat dry with paper towels and slice diagonally into thin discs.

Cut the fish into 4 slices each.

Put the squid, skin side up, on a cutting board and make very fine slits two-thirds of the way through the thickness, first lengthways, then crossways. Put in a bowl, pour over boiling water and drain. As the squid curls up, the slits open to form a flower. Immediately plunge into cold water. Pat dry with paper towels and cut into 4 bite-sized pieces.

Soak the shiitakes in warm water for 30 minutes and drain, retaining the soaking liquid. Cut off the stems and put in a saucepan with the sugar, mirin and a pinch of salt. Cover with some of the soaking liquid, stir, bring to the boil and simmer for 4–5 minutes until most of the liquid disappears. Let cool in the liquid.

Cut 2 green slices off the cucumber, 5 cm/2 inches wide. Make fine slits lengthways, leaving 1 cm/½ inch intact on one side. Open up the slits to make 2 cucumber fans.

Mix the hand vinegar ingredients in a small bowl.

Dip your fingers in the hand vinegar and divide the rice between 2 bowls and arrange the seafood over the rice and top with a cucumber fan and a pile of pink pickled ginger. Serve on small individual plates with wasabi and a little jug of soy sauce.

1 recipe vinegared rice
(see page 13)

a tub of spring sushi

radish petals

4–5 radishes, trimmed

2 tablespoons Japanese
rice vinegar

2 tablespoons sugar

This is a pretty variation of *chirashi-zushi* decorated with 'petals' made of radish and egg for a lovely finishing touch.

egg petals

1 egg, beaten with a pinch of
sea salt

¼ teaspoon cornflour/
cornstarch mixed with
a little water

sunflower oil, for frying

Cut a wedge out of each radish, then slice each radish crossways to form 5–6 petal shapes. Put the rice vinegar and sugar in a bowl and stir well until sugar has dissolved. Add the radish slices and marinate for a few hours or overnight. The red colour dissolves into the vinegar, making the slices cherry pink.

Mix the egg in a bowl with a pinch of salt and the blended cornflour. Heat a small frying pan/skillet, brush with the oil, add the egg mixture and cook until set. Using moulds or a small knife, cut out small shapes from the egg pancake such as hearts or petals.

your choice of

5 dried shiitake mushrooms

5 tablespoons/⅓ cup sugar

2½ tablespoons mirin
(sweetened Japanese rice wine)

1 teaspoon Japanese
soy sauce (shoyu)

50 ml/¼ cup chicken stock

½ carrot, sliced into 2–3 cm/
1-inch matchsticks

25 g/1 oz. mangetout/
snowpeas, trimmed

75 g/3 oz. cod fillet

1 tablespoon sake

red food colouring (optional)

3 tablespoons white sesame
seeds, lightly toasted in a dry
frying pan/skillet

200 g/8 oz. small prawns/
shrimp, peeled and
lightly cooked

sea salt

Soak the shiitakes in warm water for 30 minutes, then drain, retaining the soaking liquid. Discard the stems and thinly slice the caps crossways. Put the shiitake slices, 100 ml/½ cup from the soaking liquid and 2 tablespoons of the sugar in a saucepan, bring to the boil and cook for 3–4 minutes. Add the mirin and soy sauce, then simmer until the liquid disappears.

Put the chicken stock in a saucepan, add ½ teaspoon of the sugar, a pinch of salt and the carrot. Bring to the boil and cook for 2–3 minutes until just soft. Let cool in the juice.

Blanch the mangetout in lightly salted water. Slice diagonally into diamonds.

Bring a saucepan of water to the boil, add the cod, simmer for 3–4 minutes, then drain. Carefully remove the skin and all the bones. Return to a dry saucepan, add the sake, the remaining sugar and a pinch of salt. Using a fork, finely flake over low heat. If using red colouring, dilute it in a little water, then quickly stir to make a light pink *soboro* (fish flakes).

While the rice is still warm, fold in the shiitakes, carrot matchsticks, fish, sesame seeds and prawns. Top with the radish and egg 'petals' and serve.

flower cutters or a small
sharp knife

serves 4–6

lotus leaf rice dumplings

These pleasing rice dumplings are wrapped in lotus leaves instead of sheets of nori seaweed for a change to create a satisfying yet light snack or lunch.

370 g/2 cups sweet glutinous/
sticky rice

4 dried lotus leaves

½ teaspoon salt

1 teaspoon sesame oil

1 chicken breast, finely chopped

1 tablespoon cornflour/
cornstarch

2 teaspoons vegetable oil

4 shiitake mushrooms, sliced

1 leek, sliced

1 Chinese sausage (marinated
and smoked pork sausage
found in Chinese markets),
thinly sliced

2 teaspoons oyster sauce

2 teaspoons Japanese soy sauce
(shoyu)

1 tablespoon Shaoxing
rice wine

2 tablespoons caster/superfine
sugar

*a bamboo steamer, lined with
parchment paper*

a rice cooker

makes 8 dumplings

Rinse and drain the rice, then soak in 600 ml/2½ cups water for 2 hours.

Meanwhile, cut each folded lotus leaf in half lengthways. Submerge the leaves in hot water and leave to soak for 30 minutes, pressing down if they float up. Trim the leaves with kitchen scissors/shears until they are a similar size and trim off the hard stalk end.

Drain the rice thoroughly. In the bowl of a rice cooker, place the rice, salt, sesame oil and 250 ml/1 cup water. Cook following the packet instructions.

Mix the chopped chicken with the cornflour. Put the oil in a large frying pan/skillet over a high heat and fry the chicken for 3 minutes. Add the mushrooms, sliced leek and sausage and cook, stirring for a further few minutes. Lower the heat and add the oyster sauce, soy sauce, Shaoxing rice wine and caster/superfine sugar. Stir-fry until chicken is cooked and the vegetables are tender. Set aside to cool.

Divide the cooked rice into 8 portions. With wet fingertips, divide each portion of rice in half. Shape 8 half-portions into rectangles in the centre of each lotus leaf half. Put 1 tablespoon of chicken mixture on top and spread evenly. Top the meat with the other halves of rice to cover them completely.

Fold the bottom of the leaves up over the rice. Fold in the left and right sides, and then roll each leaf away from you towards the curved edge to make a rectangular packet. Place the dumplings seam-side down on the bamboo steamer. Steam over boiling water for 45 minutes, or until heated through. Serve warm.

japanese rice balls

Nutritionally, brown rice is superior to white rice and is a good source of fibre – it also has a lovely nutty flavour. To make these Japanese rice balls, or *onigiri*, use short-grain rice, rather than long-grain or basmati, as its sticky texture will ensure the balls hold together.

175 g/6 oz. short-grain brown rice, rinsed well

2 teaspoons black sesame seeds

2 teaspoons hulled hemp seeds

¼ teaspoon togarashi spice mix, plus extra for sprinkling (optional)

½ sheet of toasted nori seaweed, cut into 10 strips, each about 4 x 1 cm/ 1½ x ½ inch in size

sea salt, to taste

fillings (optional)

Japanese pickles, cut into small pieces

kimchi, finely chopped

smoked tofu, cut into small cubes

grated cooked egg yolk

makes 10 balls

Put the rice in a pan. Pour over 275 ml/generous 1 cup cold water (it should cover the rice by about 1 cm/½ inch) and bring to the boil. Cover the pan with a lid, turn the heat to its lowest setting, and cook for 20–25 minutes until the rice is tender and all the water has been absorbed. Turn off the heat and leave to stand for 15 minutes.

Mix together the black sesame seeds, hemp seeds and togarashi, then stir the mixture into the rice.

To make plain onigiri, take a small piece of clingfilm/plastic wrap in the palm of one hand and place 2 tablespoons of rice in the centre. Gather up the edges of the clingfilm/plastic wrap and twist the top, then gently press the rice into a triangle, ball or cylindrical shape.

To make filled onigiri, follow the instructions above. Put the rice in the centre of the clingfilm/plastic wrap and press it into a disc with wet fingers. Place a piece of pickle, kimchi, smoked tofu or ½ teaspoon of egg yolk in the centre and shape the rice around, using the clingfilm/plastic wrap to help, to encase the filling. Next, shape the rice into a triangle or ball shape.

Remove the clingfilm/plastic wrap and stick a strip of nori around the base, then finish with a sprinkling of togarashi on top, if liked. Eat straightaway or store, covered, in the fridge for up to 2 days.

stuffed squid sushi

Meat is rarely used in sushi but this sweet, dry-cooked minced meat goes well with vinegared rice. It can be eaten as it is, or use it as a stuffing for squid and serve as an unusual party canapé. If you don't like to use meat, just use the squid flaps and tentacles in the sumeshi mixture, but reduce the cooking juice accordingly.

2 medium squid, cleaned

3 tablespoons sake

2–3 tablespoons Japanese rice vinegar

2 tablespoons sugar

1 tablespoon mirin (sweetened Japanese rice wine) or sweet sherry

2 tablespoons Japanese soy sauce (shoyu)

50 g/2 oz. minced/ground chicken or beef

2.5-cm/1-inch piece fresh ginger, peeled and finely chopped

⅔ recipe vinegared rice (see page 13)

pickled ginger, to serve

makes 10–12 pieces

Peel the outer skin off the squid. It comes off easily if you hold the two flaps together and peel down the body. Put the 2 main bodies in a saucepan, add 1 tablespoon sake, cover with boiling water and simmer for 1–2 minutes. Do not overcook. Drain, rub the surface with a damp cloth to remove any marks, then sprinkle with the rice vinegar all over to retain the whiteness. Chop the flaps and tentacles.

Put the remaining sake, the sugar, mirin and soy sauce in a saucepan, mix and bring to the boil over moderate heat. Add the minced chicken or beef, the chopped squid flaps and tentacles and the chopped ginger, then stir vigorously with a fork until the meat turns white. Using a slotted spoon, transfer the cooked meat to another bowl, leaving the juice in the saucepan. Boil the juice over high heat for 1–2 minutes until thickened. Stir the meat back into the saucepan to absorb the juice and remove from the heat.

Make the vinegared rice following the method on page 13, and while still warm fold in the dry-cooked meat. Tightly stuff each squid body with half the rice mixture and, using a sharp knife, slice crossways into 5–6 pieces.

Arrange on plates and serve with pickled ginger.

index

recipe credits

Jordan Bourke
Smoked Mackerel Sushi Rolls

Maxine Clark
Smoked salmon & cucumber sushi rolls

Amy Ruth Finegold
Sesame Seared Tuna

Nicola Graimes
Japanese Rice Balls

Dunja Gulin
Vegan Sushi
Vegan Temaki Rolls

Tori Haschka
Salmon and Cucumber Bites

Emi Kazuko
A Tub of Spring Sushi
Battleship Rolls
Big Sushi Rolls
Children's Favourite Sushi
Egg Cup Sushi
Hand-moulded Sushi
Inside Out Sushi
Japanese Omelette
Lettuce Boats
Lettuce Rolls
Lunchbox Sushi
Mackerel Sushi Pieces
Omelette Parcel
Rolled Sushi Variations
Seared Tuna Sashimi Salad
Smoked Fish Sushi
Smoked Salmon Hand Rolls
Stars, Hearts and Flowers
Stuffed Squid Sushi
Sushi in a Bowl
Tofu Bags
Vinegared Rice

Loretta Liu
Lotus Leaf Rice Dumplings

Uyen Luu
Raw Fish and Chips

Elsa Peterson-Schepelern
Cucumber sushi
Sushi Cones

James Porter
'Ahi Katsu
Poke Inari Cups
Spam Musabi

Annie Rigg
Mixed Sashimi

Fiona Smith
Avocado Rolls with Chive and Cashews
Bright Vegetable and Thin Omelette
  Rolls
California Rolls
Five-Colour Roll
Fresh Oyster Roll with Chilli Cucumber
Grilled Tofu Roll
Marinated Beef Sushi
Miso-marinated Asparagus Roll
Mixed Pickles
Mushroom Omelette Sushi Roll
Pickled Courgette Roll with Beetroot
  Sashimi
Pickled Ginger
Pickled Salmon Roll
Simple Rolled Sushi
Slow-cooked Squid Sushi
Smoked Fish Hand Rolls
Spicy Tuna Roll
Sushi Balls with Roast Pork and Pickled
  Plums
Tempura Prawn Roll
Teriyaki Chicken Roll with Miso Dipping
  Sauce
Treasures of the Sea Battleship Sushi
Vinegared Mackerel and Avocado Roll
Wasabi Mayonnaise and Tuna Roll
Wasabi Paste
Yakitori Octopus Roll

Milli Taylor
Crabstick and Avocado Maki
Honey Soy Mackerel and Daikon Maki

Jenna Zoe
Quinoa Maki

photography credits

Steve Baxter
Page 126.

Peter Cassidy
Pages 2, 4–5, 6, 7 middle, 7 bottom,
8–9, 12, 14, 15, 18, 22, 23, 24–25, 27,
28, 31, 34, 46, 48, 50, 58, 70, 75, 76,
77, 88, 89, 93, 96, 97, 98, 99, 100, 102,
103, 108, 109, 110–11, 118, 124, 128,
129, 140, 142, 143, 144, 146, 147, 148,
151, 152.

Helen Cathcart
Pages 64–5.

Louie Hagger
Page 155.

Mowie Kay
Pages 81, 104, 134.

William Lingwood
Pages 54, 55, 57, 106, 117, 118.

Diana Miller
Pages 7 top, 10, 16, 19, 20, 32, 35, 36,
38, 39, 40, 43, 44, 47, 51, 52, 56, 59,
60, 61, 68, 73, 74, 82, 86, 91, 92, 95,
113, 114.

Noel Murphy
Page 67.

William Reavell
Page 85.

Toby Scott
Page 121.

Simon Walton
Page 116.

Isobel Weld
Page 133.

Kate Whittaker
Pages 72, 78.

Clare Winfield
Pages 122, 130, 137, 138, 156.